DEPARTURES AND ARRIVALS

DEPARTURES
AND
ARRIVALS

ERIC NEWBY

HarperCollins*Publishers*

HarperCollins*Publishers*
77–85 Fulham Palace Road,
Hammersmith, London w6 8jb

Published by HarperCollins*Publishers* 1999
1 3 5 7 9 8 6 4 2

A catalogue record for this book is
available from the British Library

ISBN 0 00 255621 9

Set in PostScript Linotype Minion by
Rowland Phototypesetting Ltd,
Bury St Edmunds, Suffolk

Printed and bound in Great Britain by
Caledonian International Book Manufacturing Ltd, Glasgow

To Wanda with love

Many thanks to Lucinda McNeile and Kate Morris
for all their help

CONTENTS

ILLUSTRATIONS

Between pages 50 and 51

Departures
Wanda and Sonia Newby in Barnes
The Newbys, 1963
The Orient Express near Çorlu
Eric Newby in Parachilna, Australia
Coober Pedy, Australia
A Gothic folly at Bindon Abbey, Dorset
Wanda among the ruins at Palmyra
Camels in Northern Rajasthan
The Palio
Elephant bathing, India

Between pages 146 and 147

Eric Newby in the Cheviot Hills
Cycling along the Canal de L'Ourcq
Graffiti at the Canal de L'Ourcq
The coast of southern Turkey
A shepherd in Pamukkale, Anatolia
The *peri bacalari*, or fairy chimneys, of Anatolia
Eric Newby in Tiananmen Square
The palace of the Imam Yahya, Yemen
The Salt Souk, Yemen
St Aldhelm's Head, seen from Swyre Head
The Roman Catholic chapel in the grounds of Lulworth Castle
West Bucknowle, Dorset

INTRODUCTION

WHATEVER ELSE we remember of our travels, we remember our departures and arrivals. Often they are the most enduring of all our memories of them. In 1963, together with Wanda, my wife, I embarked on the Ganges in an open boat to row from the foothills of the Himalayas to the Indian Ocean. Some 200 metres from our starting point, from which we had been seen off by an old man who dropped sacred sweets on us as provisions for the journey, and some 1,900 kilometres short of our destination in the Bay of Bengal, the boat grounded in some 40 centimetres of water which proved to be the uniform depth of the Ganges at this season at this point, and it took five-and-a-half days to cover the next 56 kilometres, mostly by pushing it.

Nothing in the course of the entire trip, which took three months to accomplish, left such an indelible imprint on our minds as the moment when we discovered that the Ganges was only 40 centimetres deep and that our boat drew 46 centimetres when loaded.

To depart is often more satisfying than to arrive unless you are the first on the scene. Nothing was more deflationary to Scott and his companions than to find that they were the second party to reach the South Pole. Would I have set off at all if I had known what the journey would be like or what I was going to find at my destination are questions I have often asked myself, reminded of the wartime poster which read 'Don't waste food! Why did you take it if you weren't going to eat it?' To which some wit added a codicil: 'I didn't know it was going to taste like this!'

For years explorers attempted to reach Timbuktu, the mysterious city on the edge of the Sahara that, ever since the twelfth century, had been the hub of the North African world, and in which salt had been traded for the seemingly inexhaustible gold of Guinea, a city in which, according to the Muslim traveller Leo Africanus, who visited it in 1526, there were plates and sceptres of solid gold 'some whereof weigh 1,300 pounds'.

The first-known European to reach Timbuktu and return in one piece was Réné Caillié, a penniless young Frenchman who had been inspired to become an explorer by reading *Robinson Crusoe*. Too late to see it in its heyday – the trade in gold had more or less come to an end – he reached the fabled city after a terrifyingly dangerous journey on 20 April 1828. 'I looked around,' he wrote, 'and found the sight before me did not answer my expectations of Timbuktu. The city presented, at first view, nothing but a mass of ill-looking houses, built of earth. Nothing was to be seen in all directions but immense plains of quicksand of a yellowish-white colour.'

No one *really* enjoys arriving anywhere by train. (Nor does anyone in their right mind enjoy departing or arriving by plane, with the possible exception of the pilot whose toy it is.) Will there be any porters? Will there be any trolleys for the luggage if there aren't? Will there be any taxis? Will they be fitted with meters? These and similar questions that even the most hardened travellers ask themselves as the train comes into the platform all help to contribute to the particular form of *angst*, the generally non-specific but nonetheless acute form of anxiety described by Cyril Connolly (disguised under the *nom de plume* Palinurus) in *The Unquiet Grave* as the *Angoisse des Gares*, the Agony of the Stations: 'Bad when we meet someone at the station, much worse when we are seeing them off; not present when departing oneself, but unbearable when arriving . . .'

The best arrivals are by sea, that is unless your engine has broken down and the Cliffs of Moher are a lee shore. The first sight of a great city from the sea is big medicine, powerful magic, unforgettable, however much of a let-down it may prove to be on closer acquaintance. New York seen from the Hudson in the early morning with the sun roaring up over the East River turning the tall buildings into gigantic Roman candles; Venice as your vessel runs in through the Porto di Lido into St Mark's Basin with the domes and campaniles liquefying and reconstituting themselves in the mirage; Istanbul as your ship comes up the Marmara and sweeps round Seraglio Point towards the Golden Horn and you see silhouetted against the evening sky the fantastic, improbable, incomparable skyline of Old Stamboul.

It is not only the great cities that have this effect on the arriving traveller. This is how T. E. Lawrence described his first sight of Jidda, the then little port of Mecca, seen from the deck of a passenger ship in the Red Sea while he was on his way to meet the leaders of the Arab Revolt in 1917: 'When at last we anchored in the outer harbour off the white town, between the blazing sky and its reflection in the mirage which swept and rolled over the wide lagoon, then the heat of Arabia came out like a drawn sword and struck us speechless . . . There were only lights and shadows, the white and black gaps of streets: in front, the pallid lustre of the haze shimmering upon the inner harbour; behind, the dazzle of league after league of featureless sand running up to an edge of low hills, faintly suggested in the far away mist and heat.'

It is these and similar vistas, whether wild or civilized, that make one want to shout 'How beautiful the world is!', that made an elderly lady of my acquaintance, when taken on an outing from her native village in the Po Valley which she had never previously left, cry on arriving on the watershed of the Apennines from which there was an extensive view, '*Com'è grande il mondo!*' . . . 'How big the world is!' . . . and insist on being taken home.

Up to Ther Bend and Back

CASTELNAU MANSIONS, BARNES, SW13, the block of flats in which I was born, in 1919, on the south side of Hammersmith Bridge, was one of several such blocks built in the 1900s on what had been marshland and open country.

Our flat was on the first floor – Three Ther Mansions, as it was known to the tradesmen who sent their delivery boys out on bicycles from the nearby shops to deliver my mother's orders. And it had what the estate agents used to describe in the twenties as 'commanding extensive and splendid views over the Metropolitan Water Board's Reservoir and Filter Beds'. The filter beds were lovely, full of golden sand that I longed to play with, but was never able to do so as they were fenced in.

Castelnau, the main road which separated our block of flats from the reservoir, was and is the almost dead-straight road which runs from Hammersmith Bridge to the pub called until recently the Red Lion, and, although it is only about a mile long, it appears to be much longer. It was built in 1827, at the same time as the original Hammersmith Suspension Bridge, a beautiful, slender structure designed by William Tierney Clarke. In 1887 it was replaced by another suspension bridge of cast-iron, a rather elephantine structure designed by Sir Joseph Bazalgette, the man who designed the London sewers. (The IRA tried to blow it up in 1939, but was thwarted when a heroic passer-by picked up the bomb and threw it into the river.) The street was named Castelnau after the family seat of the Boileau family, Castelnau de la Gard at Nîmes, the head of the family being a General de Castelnau.

The Boileau family also had a house by the Thames at Mortlake, upstream from Barnes. In fact the family must be still turning in their graves to hear their beautiful street called 'Castlenore', and the Boileau

Arms, the handsome pub at the bridge end of it, built in 1842, 'Ther Boiler'.

Castelnau has only one almost imperceptible kink in its entire length, again known to almost everyone as 'Ther Bend', which effectively prevents anyone from looking up or down its entire length from either end, except from the top of a bus.

'We'll just walk up to Ther Bend and back,' my mother would suddenly say when I no longer had a nurse and was too old to travel by mail cart – which my nurse pushed while I sat looking ahead with my back to the engine.

And we used to set off for this short walk up Castelnau, something less than half a mile, suitably clad against the elements, which were as unpredictable in Barnes as anywhere else.

Facing our front door on the same landing as ours, which was the only place for me to play when it rained, was Number Four. It was occupied by a friend of my mother's. A jolly, long-legged dress-buyer at Derry and Toms, the large department store in Kensington High Street. She loved parties.

She was known to me as 'Auntie Lil' and she had been installed in Number Four by her friend, to me a rather elderly dentist who had his practice in an elegant little house behind Kensington Church Street. He was known to me as 'Uncle Max'. I wasn't as keen on Uncle Max as I was on Auntie Lil, as he was also my dentist and not surprisingly I associated him with pain. But 'Auntie Lil' was all right, and she gave me bars of Fry's Chocolate Cream to munch, which made more visits to Uncle Max inevitable.

On the whole things were not going well at Number Four. Then Uncle Max left Auntie Lil, and I remember a good deal of wailing taking place while she was being comforted by my mother; but she still stayed on at Number Four, and then, some time later, she went away. I missed Auntie Lil, and her Fry's Chocolate Cream bars.

The descent to the ground floor, where One and Two were to be found, was by a linoleum-covered staircase with shiny wooden banisters, down which I used to slide. In fact I could slide the whole way down the banisters from the topmost floor to the ground floor, if so inclined.

The only other occupants of the flats on the upper floors I knew were a Hindu doctor named Dr Wallah and his Scottish nurse/girlfriend. Dr

Wallah bore a striking resemblance to Gandhi in early life (in South Africa), but both were so desperately shy that it was difficult for even a five-year-old to talk to them.

Down on the ground floor Number One The Mansions was occupied by Mr and Mrs Ludovici. She was called Marie, was French and clever. He was partly Italian and known to his friends as Ludo. He was something pretty important in the Goldsmiths and Silversmiths Company in Regent Street, and had dealings with Indian princes. He went to work each day by taxi, dressed in a double-breasted black jacket, striped trousers, starched white collar and cuffs, and he always wore a clove carnation in his buttonhole, supplied by a florist near the Boileau Arms. Neither Mr nor Mrs Ludovici suffered fools, and/or small boys, gladly or ungladly and I wouldn't have dared call them Uncle Ludo or Auntie Marie for all the tea in China.

Although posher than the Newbys, the Ludovicis, I was pleased to note, had a much poorer view of the reservoir than we did on the first floor of The Mansions, due to a privet hedge in front of their windows having been allowed to grow to an excessive height. In fact they couldn't see the reservoir at all. Perhaps they were the sort of people who didn't care for views of reservoirs.

Down here on the ground floor there was a space under the stairs in which my chained-up mail cart had been parked until recently, still awaiting my parents' decision as to how to dispose of it. Eventually, they bequeathed it to a tramp – what was then known as 'a gentleman of the road' – who was on his way to spend the summer in the vicinity of Penzance but had got blown slightly off course. He said it would be invaluable to him for carrying his gear when sleeping rough in the open. At that time the main roads of Britain were full of tramps, many of them ex-soldiers on their way southwards to the sun, or else, in winter, travelling from one workhouse to another. There were even some women tramps, but they were rather more frightening than the men. Our particular tramp was about forty and had been a corporal in a Rifle Regiment. He was smart as tramps go, but when he left us, pushing what was now his mail cart, after having transferred his possessions to it from a sack and after a slice of fruit cake and a nice cup of hot sweet tea, the following day we found some strange, cabbalistic chalk marks on the wall outside the entrance, which I later learned years later was tramps' language to the effect that the occupants of Number Three were a decent touch; but none ever came to try us out.

Now, down on the ground floor, we pushed open the main door, which had a glittering pair of brass doorknobs on it, polished by Edwards, the Head Porter, an ex-Guardsman. He was the custodian of all the flats which belonged to the London County Freehold and Leasehold Company. He was also in command of a number of lesser staff – some of them ex-soldiers who limped, having been wounded. They performed more menial functions, mostly in connection with dustbins and their contents. Edwards also polished the buttons on his navy blue tailcoat, using a button stick to prevent the polish getting on the material. Fifteen years later, when I joined the Army, in 1939, I also found myself using a button stick.

And now, out in the front garden of The Mansions, where the hedges were too high to see over, we turned left on to Castelnau for the long walk up to Ther Bend. Well, it seemed long when you were only five.

On our right now was Glentham Road, at that time a working-class street which encompassed the only part of Barnes at the Hammersmith Bridge end that boasted a bit of downhill. In it was the Sunlight Laundry, which took in our washing and employed numbers of cheerful, noisy girls from Hammersmith. This was the street, too, in which my parents' chauffeur, Mr Lewington, lived, and where he kept our car, an open Citroën, in his garage. Beyond it was Fanny Road (now renamed St Hilda's Road). It was to be years later, long after the war began, and I was abroad, before anyone living in Barnes found anything remotely funny in the name Fanny in association with a road. That was, until the Americans arrived in Britain in 1942/3. They had somewhat different ideas of what a Fanny was and when they saw Fanny inscribed on a street sign, they fell about. Soon, Americans from as far away as Piccadilly Circus began making pilgrimages to Fanny Road, sw13, on the Number 9 bus.

Then we used to go on, my mother and I, past where the shops began; past the butcher's and Hewett's Stores, which had dead ducks, and geese and pheasants, partridges and grouse, all hanging outside on hooks, in due season.

And inside, dressed in white, and wearing a straw boater whatever the season, was Mr Hewett who never failed to stop doing whatever he

was doing, to doff his boater to my mother, a customer of some importance, as she sailed past with or without me in tow.

And next to Hewett's there was the chemist's, which I liked just about
as much as Uncle Fitz's surgery, as it had a wealth of what I called
'Nasty Things' on offer. And next to that there was a haberdasher's full
of boxes bursting with mother-of-pearl buttons and knicker elastic –
important when large numbers of ladies kept their handkerchiefs somewhere in their knickers; and there were rolls of lace that kept on
unrolling.

This very dark, even then very old-fashioned shop, was run by a pair
of what at that time were quite young people. They were still operating
after the Second World War, by that time incredibly bent and ancient.
They hardly ever spoke, except to say how much the bill came to, and
transacted their business with all the animation of a slow-motion film
of a ritual. I was frightened of them, all dressed in black.

The next roads on our left, opposite Ther Boiler, were Arundel Terrace
and Merthyr Terrace, which led away down to more reservoirs and
more filter beds – this end of Barnes had more water than land in it.
It was also the road that led to the council allotments, one of which
Wanda put in for as soon as she came to live in Barnes, the scourge of
the pensioners who predicted that everything she planted would come
to a sticky end. 'All that foreign stuff won't do 'ere,' they prognosticated
when she started planting 'foreign stuff' in appreciable quantities – all
of which did marvels, much to their disgust.

On the corner of Merthyr Terrace there was a dairy with a plaster of
Paris – well, it looked like plaster of Paris – cow in the window, and
walls tiled with dairy scenes. Here, on the premises, fresh-faced girls
dispensed the beverage and the milkmen delivered it to their customers
from churns loaded on to horse-drawn carts.

On the opposite side of the road there was Ther Boiler. Behind it
was then, and for years to come, open country. There was a farm – it
must have been one of the nearest farms to the centre of London –
which employed numbers of women as casual labourers. When lifting
potatoes, or whatever, they worked in all weathers short of a downpour,
and they wore sacks as aprons and over their shoulders, and men's caps.
They, too, came over the river from Hammersmith, but they were much
tougher than the girls at the Sunlight Laundry. And there was the

fishmonger's, and the Post Office and a florist's and the newsagent.

The last shop on our side of Castelnau was an ironmonger's, otherwise the Oil Shop. It was painted green and had two massive amphorae over the front of it of the sort that in Mediterranean lands are used to store olive oil, which here were painted a vivid, pillar-box red.

A short distance up towards Ther Bend was the Holy Trinity church, a rather sad, perpendicular construction of 1868, a not altogether auspicious time for building churches.

I never liked it, nor did I like the Church Hall, the scene of an unsuccessful attempt to 'interfere' with me by a bun-faced curate when I was a member of the Wolf Cub pack. The interference only amounted to my being bounced up and down on his knee but I didn't enjoy it, as I felt that I was too old to be bounced up and down on peoples' knees, and I told my mother and she told my father, and my father told the vicar and the curate was sent away to wherever curates who tried to 'interfere' with Wolf Cubs went at that time.

Near the church during the Second World War there had been an air raid shelter which had received a direct hit by a German rocket at a time when it had been filled with local inhabitants.

Here, on the opposite side of Castelnau to the church, were the premises of Boon and Porter, motor-car salesmen. The most memorable feature of Boon and Porter was an enormous advertisement for French Amilcars painted on a brick wall a couple of storeys high. It showed them roaring round a steep bank, driven by what looked like Michelin Men.

As we approached Ther Bend the houses became progressively finer, the best of all beginning at Ther Bend itself. They were semi-detached brick and stucco residences known as Castelnau Villas, built in 1842, the earliest early Victorian, with coach houses to match, and shaded by noble trees. Even to my five-year-old mind the Villas made the Mansions and the Gardens look a bit feeble – the epitome of an elegance that has rarely been repeated.

What my mother and I most enjoyed about going up to Ther Bend was that it was there that two members of the Constabulary operated what were known as 'Speed Traps'.

These constables were always the same ones. Both had identical bushy moustaches and both were fat and had very red faces. They could have been twins. When they saw with the aid of binoculars a car coming up Castelnau from the direction of Hammersmith Bridge that in their opinion was exceeding the speed limit, which at that time, in the twenties, was only twenty miles an hour, they rushed out of their hiding place behind one of the massive gate posts of Number 122 Castelnau Villas at Ther Bend blowing their whistles and waving a large red flag at the offending motorist. This dramatic event, which we looked forward to witnessing, invariably took place at three o'clock in the afternoon, by which time they had, presumably, digested their 'dinner'.

On one occasion they flagged down a Rolls-Royce, the sort in which the chauffeur is isolated from the passengers and exposed to the elements.

They, the constables, were happily engaged in taking down the chauffeur's particulars when a very small, open motor car driven by a very boozy-looking man came round Ther Bend at about sixty miles an hour, roaring with laughter and thumbing his nose at the constables who had no chance of flagging him down, let alone taking down his particulars.

And it was always at this point, at Number 122 that we turned back. Beyond it was *terra incognita* so far as my mother was concerned.

Later, when I was given a scooter, I was allowed to scoot up the footpath from our flat past Number 122 to Number 54 Castelnau alone. Number 54 was, and still is, an Edwardian house equipped with bargeboards and decked with finials; one of a whole lot of similar houses which extended southwards on both sides of the road as far as the Red Lion, a pub with a rampant lion over the entrance. Number 54 was the house of a Jewish family called Rosenthal. Their youngest son, Martin, was my best friend when we were both at a pre-prep school run by two impressive ladies in yet another Edwardian house called Castelnau College, and later at Colet Court, the prep school for St Paul's and after that at St Paul's which were opposite one another in Hammersmith Road. Mr Rosenthal, who was very all there, had worked for many years with the East Africa Company, which had laid the foundations of what are now Kenya and Uganda. Mr Rosenthal had been an intimate friend of Trader Horn, otherwise Alfred Aloysius Smith, whose reminiscences of Darkest Africa (edited by Ethelreda Lewis) had become a best-seller. Both Martin's father and Trader Horn were heroes to us. The only trouble was that neither of us had ever set eyes on Trader Horn; but Martin very kindly said that I could pretend that I knew Trader Horn, which was what he was going to do. We soon found out that if anyone asked you, 'I say, man, do you know Trader Horn?' and you said yes, you were assured of social success at Colet Court, something which, up to then, Martin and myself had stood in real need. The Rosenthal house was full of African memorabilia – the very walls groaned under the weight of huge guns for slaying elephants, dinner gongs made from elephants' tusks waiting to be banged, and the skins and heads of wild animals.

The adult Rosenthals played bridge incessantly, usually with other Jewish families to whom they were linked by marriage. Most of them lived in the same sort of houses as the Rosenthals. One of the younger sons who was about the same age as Martin and myself used to charge his mother half a crown to kiss him goodnight; but he made up for this when the war came by joining a gunner regiment and getting killed in Tunisia.

One of these families had a business in Hammersmith market. When they played bridge all of them sat at little card tables and the ladies were very elegant and made up, and whatever the weather outside – it could be a day of blazing heat – it was with the blinds drawn and the lights on. Too young to play bridge, we played *vingt-et-un* with the family's ex-nurse, a rather forbidding woman of indeterminate age called Edith, and Martin's younger sister Eva, and anyone else who could be roped in to form a quorum for a game. We ate matzos and Gentleman's Relish, an unsuitable summer snack, while the atmosphere became more and more insupportable as the men puffed away on their big cigars. It was as someone from the Christian world outside that I attended Martin's bar-mitzvah and the celebration of the Passover.

The Rosenthals had a garden large enough to play cricket in with a tennis ball which was always getting hit out of bounds, over the banks of the reservoir at the bottom of the garden. When it did we used to squeeze through an iron fence and climb the bank in order to look for the ball, but generally speaking it could be seen bobbing about out on the water and we had to wait for the wind to blow it back towards the wall of the reservoir. Usually it blew in the wrong direction and someone else picked it up, so we never saw it again. This was the biggest reservoir in Barnes, which was a wonderful sight in winter when birds from the far north congregated on it in astonishing numbers.

Sometimes, at the age of about seven or eight, when we got bored, we used to play 'rude' games together in one of the bathrooms, and on one occasion when playing 'Doctors' we gave one another a soap and water enema using a garden syringe that happened to be handy. Martin's attempt to give me one was a failure but mine to give him one had spectacular results. We were discovered by Edith who gave us a good smacking and I was sent home for the day, but she never told the Rosenthals and I continued to be invited to their house. After this we gave up 'rude' games as being injurious to health.

Although the various blocks of flats – Castelnau Mansions, Riverview Gardens, Castelnau Gardens – presented a series of fairly prosperous façades to the outside world, kept up by Mr Edwards' knob-polishing, from their backs they gave a somewhat different impression. In fact some of them bore a distinct resemblance to the slum tenements on the Hammersmith side of the river, past which I used to battle my way to Colet Court.

For example, Castelnau Mansions had several flights of steep, unlit, narrow backstairs with a very primitive privy on each landing but no washing facilities, intended for the use of domestic servants, who also had a minute bedroom next to the kitchen in each flat. Whether it was intended that the domestics should use these backstairs facilities was not clear. Our domestics never used them – they shared the bathroom and loo with us. In all the forty years my parents lived at Three Ther Mansions, these backstairs were never painted. In some other blocks of flats the occupants had to put their dustbins into lifts and lower them away down to the ground floor, where again the porters and the dustmen took over.

And behind our block there was a sad-looking garden that was no one's responsibility, with patches of grass that looked as if they had lost the race and innumerable docks that hadn't and a wooden shed. This garden led away into a series of alleys smelling of cats in which the dustbins were stacked up by the porters awaiting the arrival of the dustmen.

All in all it was a good place for children, who loved it. Fortunately, although I was an only child and the only one in Castelnau Mansions, there were others in other blocks such as Riverview Gardens, some of whom had already formed a gang, which Martin and I were invited to join, which wasn't difficult as there was no leader because everyone wanted to be leader.

The gang included Philip Turgle, who was Belgian – goodness knows how the Belgians pronounced his name; and there was Roderick Blaine ('Roderick Blaine had a Pain and it wouldn't go away again/Tee-hee!' we used to chant mindlessly). And there was Twinkle, who was American Jewish and whose father was a tailor. And there were one or two others, whose names I have forgotten. And last but not least there was Margaret Evans, the only girl in the gang, who could do anything that boys could and was braver.

It wasn't much of a gang, really, because there weren't any other such gangs in the neighbourhood, except those in Hammersmith, on the other side of the river, which were solidly working-class and dangerous whereas ours were solidly middle-class and feeble.

So we fought imaginary battles with one another in the noisome back alleyways, pretending they were trenches, and bombed one another with clay bombs which we began to manufacture when Twinkle discovered an almost endless sticky supply of the stuff in one of the back alleys. (How Twinkle came by his name was a mystery, for he was really a quite outstandingly ugly little boy.) Then we found that we could launch the bombs from the end of a nice, springy sapling; they went twice as far as they did when you simply threw them by hand.

Then we started baking the bombs over a fire made with old boxes, in order to produce a shrapnel effect, and ended up by breaking someone's kitchen window on an upper storey of a flat in Riverview Gardens. And that was the end of clay bombs.

Every so often in the winter there were thick, pea soup type fogs which sometimes lasted for days and brought London to a halt. Knowing how lethal these fogs were, it seems incredible that our parents let us out to play in them, but they did.

And when it snowed we snowballed one another, which was a good deal less painful than being clay-bombed. And on 5 November we attempted to blow ourselves to smithereens, using what were then really powerful fireworks. And when there was a spring tide we got our feet wet on the towpath. And when it was Boat Race Day, we bought what were called 'Favours' – crossed oars made of bamboo decorated with light or dark blue ribbons – from men and women who had been selling them on Boat Race Day from the year dot. And on the towpath there were scenes of Hogarthian strangeness with men chewing glass for a consideration, and drunks male and female being carted off by policemen. I was for Oxford, I thought Cambridge's light blue sissy, and for years and years Oxford never won, testing my loyalty.

It was when one of the great fogs enveloped London that, equipped with a single lantern containing a single candle, and with scarves wrapped round our mouths to stop the fog getting in, we braved the pitchest of pitch-darkness down in the central heating tunnels that ran under the flats at the bottom end of Riverview Gardens, the ones with a view over the river, in which red-sailed Thames barges could still be seen going down on the ebb tide. At that time it was not a very salubrious situation. Facing the flats on the left bank of the river was the huge refinery of Manbre and Garton – the smells that emanated from it owed more to saccharine than sugar and at times the whole area reeked of it. A little further upstream towards Hammersmith Bridge were the Hammersmith Borough Council's tips, where all the rubbish was shot into lighters and taken away down the river – that is the parts of it that were not blown across the river and over Riverview Gardens in the form of thick clouds of dust.

Down there in the tunnels all of us were frightened, except Margaret Evans who told us not to be 'funky'. Down there in the tunnels there was not a sound except for an occasional clonking noise from the heating system. Down there we were looking for the spookiest place in Riverview Gardens and this was it. But the most memorable time for our gang was when my mother, who liked the idea of a gang, rigged us out as ghosts, using old dust sheets. Dressed all in white, with tall, conical hats stuffed with tissue paper to keep them upright and slits for eyeholes, we looked like miniature members of the Ku-Klux-Klan, or penitents in Holy Week.

Wearing these outfits, we used to swoop down The Gardens, making ghastly ghostly noises, alarming the inhabitants of the flats and gesticulating at the passengers on the upper decks of the Number 9 buses.

By the time I married Wanda in Florence in 1946, I had already lived for nearly twenty years in Castelnau Mansions and I felt that I had had enough of it. Already, by the time I was nine or ten and was at Colet

Court, the alleyways that had served as trenches in which we played our war games, pelting one another with clay bombs of varying degrees of hardness, now seemed nothing less than squalid, and the smell of dustbins and cats insupportable. And with all this against it our gang simply melted away, and the whole tiny area became intolerably sad.

I made what I now see to have been two attempts to get away from Castelnau Mansions, the first in 1938, when I became a sailor, the second in 1939 when I became a soldier. Both times I found myself inexorably drawn back to them. Even when Wanda came to England in 1947 and we had to find somewhere to live, we had to stay with my parents at Three Ther Mansions. They were heroic because the flat was pretty small for four of us. There was a double bedroom which just took a double bed, with views down The Gardens to the astonishing great hulk of Harrods Furniture Repository, a single bedroom, which had been mine, a small drawing-room and dining-room, both overlooking the reservoir, a very small hall and a minute bathroom. And there was a kitchen and the minute domestic's bedroom, which my father kept his suits in as there was no living-in domestic any more. And in it he also kept, done up with string, hundreds of back copies of the *Morning Post*. And there was the terrible loo on the backstairs.

Why my parents, who were only badly off intermittently up to that time, chose to live in such crowded quarters when there was no need for them to do so was a mystery to me. I can only think that they weren't really interested in homes in the accepted sense of the word at all. Years of rag-trade travelling, anywhere from Bradford to Berlin and Perth to Paris, where they bought 'models' to copy, most of the time living in hotels, with all the advantages of having room service at the press of a button and not having to make beds, may have blunted their taste for the homely hearth. Whether this was true or not they used to spend several months of the year travelling, which seemed like whole ages to me.

It could have been worse. They left me in the care of a housekeeper, a Miss Roy, a good, kind woman whose Liverpudlian accent I used to try and copy, and of whom I was very fond, so that I could not have had any real need to be sorry when my parents set off on what they called 'The Journey' in order to sell their productions, something that I was to set off on some twenty years later. Nevertheless, I always found myself crying as they went down the stairs and through the door with the brass doorknobs to the taxi waiting outside The Mansions, wondering if I would ever see them again.

Travels with a Baby

·⟨❄⟩·

In January 1947 the British coal industry was nationalized and in one of the coldest winters anyone could remember there was no coal. In these inauspicious circumstances Wanda gave birth to a daughter in Queen Charlotte's Maternity Hospital across the river near Stamford Brook. At that time we were living in a small, top floor flat round the corner from Three Ther Mansions at 24 Castelnau Gardens, for which we paid what seemed the high rent of £63 a year. If anyone thinks that life with Wanda was dull in that flat, or later, when we lived in Riverview Gardens, then they have got it all wrong. It was in Castelnau Gardens that she let slip a can full of garbage which she was trying to insert into one of the lifts on an upper floor of the building – it fell on one of the porters down below. He didn't sue us. It was a miracle. Later, in Riverview Gardens, she forgot to turn the gas off. This led to a spectacular explosion which destroyed a stuffed fish; but not as spectacular as the one when she boiled a kettle full of methylated spirits, under the impression that it was water, while camping on the banks of the Somme en route for Italy.

In the summer of 1947, when the baby was about seven months old, Wanda decided to take her to visit her parents who lived in the Carso, the strange limestone country around Trieste, leaving me to get on with the execution of the autumn orders, some of which we would soon be delivering to the shops. At the time I was working for the family firm as a commercial traveller in the fashion business.

Although she had been very reluctant to do so, being of an economical turn of mind, she had eventually been persuaded to travel by wagon-lit. At this period, with large areas of Europe still in a state bordering on chaos, it seemed a justifiable extravagance for a woman travelling alone with a baby.

I had also arranged for her to travel in a through coach from Calais, which meant that when the train reached the Gare du Nord, instead of getting down there and taking a taxi across Paris to the Gare de Lyon, she could remain on board and be shunted round the city on what is known as the Ceinture to the Gare de Lyon, where it would be attached to the Simplon-Orient Express.

I got the two of them to Victoria in good time for the boat train to Dover, in our Hillman Minx; but as we were walking to the platform preceded by a porter pushing the remainder of her luggage and with the baby swinging between us in a portable cot, Wanda suddenly said, 'I've forgotten the basket!'

The last time I had seen the basket was in the hall of the flat. It contained all the mysterious necessities of weaned-baby travel, many of which I had myself regarded as mandatory when I was a baby – huge quantities of nappies, boiled water and a complete menu of baby food and drink for three days on a train. The extra day's supply was in case the train broke down. At that time, with the war only recently over, baby food was not so easily obtained in Europe as it is today and Wanda had prepared purées of fresh vegetables and farmyard chicken, none of them out of tins. 'Where I come from,' Wanda said, 'we don't give babies tings from tins.'

'Hurruck,' she said, which at that time was still the nearest she could get to a correct pronunciation of my Christian name, having considered the implications, 'I must have zat basket.'

In 1947 traffic in London was not yet the problem that it was shortly to become. In fact it was perhaps less dense than it had been before the war. I had something like half an hour to get to Hammersmith Bridge from Victoria and back again before the train left; but in spite of everything en route being in my favour I arrived back at the station with the basket just in time to see the end of the train disappear beyond the end of the platform. I asked for an interview with the Stationmaster and explained the situation to him. He was dressed in a morning coat and black top hat, having just seen off some distinguished personage by the same train. 'That's a bad business,' he said. 'You can't have a baby eating all sorts of messed-up foreign stuff, I can see that.' And he busied himself with the telephone, but to no avail.

'We can't stop the boat train,' he said. 'It's not as easy as that. I wish

I could send an engine after it but we can't do that either and, anyway, it would never catch it up,' which evoked memories of Mr Toad being pursued by an engine-load of beefeaters and policemen all shouting at the tops of their voices 'Stop, Stop, Stop!'

'Have you thought of the air?' he said finally, speaking of it as it must have seemed to him, an unfamiliar element from another world. 'Why not try the air? Ring up the airline people. You can use my telephone.'

On the telephone, however, I was once more a man of no account, a man without qualities – 'I am speaking from the office of the Stationmaster at Victoria Station' cut little ice with the man I was speaking to at the airline's office, who was soon convinced when I unfolded my problem to him that he was dealing with a lunatic. And it became obvious that the only thing to do was to go to their office, taking the basket with me, which I did.

There I was told that if the basket was to stand any chance of getting to Paris that day I would have to take it to the airport myself, and hand it in to the Air Freight office there in person.

I suddenly remembered that I had an appointment to show evening dresses to the model dress-buyer at Harrods, an appointment which I had only been able to make with great difficulty and exertion; but by this time the problem of the basket had begun to exercise such an obsessive fascination over me that any sense of proportion I might have possessed had vanished.

'Pity,' she said when I telephoned her to tell her what had happened, and could I possibly come tomorrow. 'I'm finishing up here this morning and going on holiday this afternoon.'

What I ought to have done was to have taken the dresses to Harrods, and shown them to her. She was in fact fascinated by the dilemma I was in and I would probably have got an order. Once in the store I could have contacted the manager of the Food Hall as an account customer, although a not very important one, and persuaded him to telephone Paris and ask some caterer, such as Fauchon in the Place de la Madeleine, to deliver a hamper of food suitable for infants to the Gare de Lyon. Instead I rashly took it upon myself to see whether I could get a basket of baby food from London to Paris by air.

It was midday before I got to what was then London's embryonic airport. At that time it consisted of a number of dreary-looking huts, which gave incoming passengers the sensation of arriving in some beleaguered fortress and those taking off the sensation of leaving one.

In a hut occupied by 'Air Freight' I began to fill in a declaration form, writing 'Baby Food, etc.' under *Contents*. Dire penalties were threatened for any misinformation I might give.

''Ullo, 'ullo, what's this – baby food?' said a gloomy-looking man – almost everyone was gloomy in 1947, the promised land being still just around the corner. 'Got an Export Licence?'

'Export Licence?'

'Yur, Export Licence. Board of Trade. It's food. You need an Export Licence for Food. Two kinds of licence, Specific and Bulk. You need a Specific.'

'No one told me. Where can I get one? Can you give me one?'

'Theobald's Road.'

'Where's that?'

'In the City.'

Finally, having cut me down to what he estimated was my appropriate size, he relented and allowed me to fill in Form 91b, relating to 'Export of Specific Articles of Food to the Scheduled Territories' I think it was, which he kept up his sleeve he told me, as he became more genial, for just such emergencies as this – that is if any similar emergency could be envisaged.

Now things began to look up. I fell into the hands of what at that time was still referred to as 'a good type', one with a large RAF moustache, and what was more important with a human being behind it. And I began to see that my fortunes or lack of them were developing a kind of rhythm that if expressed graphically would look like one of those wildly fluctuating temperature charts which are suspended over the patients' beds in funny cartoons about hospitals. First I forgot the basket. Then I got it. Then I missed the train. Then I met a nice stationmaster and so on, and now I was being helped by a nice man with a huge moustache.

'Hm,' he said. 'You've had a rotten day so far by the sound of it. Let's see what time the Simplon-Orient leaves the Gare de Lyon. George, ring up Victoria, Continental Enquiries, on that special number, otherwise you'll never get through, and find out what time the Simplon-Orient leaves the Gare de Lyon tonight, French time . . . No good at the Gare du Nord, she's on the Ceinture in a through coach . . . Leaves the Gare de Lyon at 21.05, French time . . . Right, I'll ring Le Bourget' – and to me: 'You don't happen to have the *voiture* number and the compartment, do you?. Pity . . . Hallo, Armand . . . I know . . . Well, you'll have to . . . That's right, send Alphonse, by motor cycle. He can hand the basket to the *Chef de Train* personally.'

'One of our best men,' he said as he put down the receiver, 'Alphonse. He was a courier in the Resistance up near the Belfort Gap. Unfortunately there's no plane until this evening and I can't risk sending it by passenger plane for reasons which I don't want to bore you with. But don't worry, he should just make it. Between ourselves if we charged you for all this it would cost you a fortune. As it is, have it with our compliments.'

When I finally reached Great Marlborough Street, my parents' London premises, later in the afternoon I was handed a telegram. It had been sent from Dover Harbour and read: 'Don't send basket. Wanda.'

This is what subsequently happened to it. It reached Le Bourget but the plane was late and Alphonse, hero of the Resistance, whirled it to the Gare de Lyon on his motor cycle a bare eight minutes before the Simplon-Orient pulled out. Owing to a clerical error, none of the boards displayed outside the wagons-lits which gave the passengers' names had Wanda's name on it and the *Chef de Train* disclaimed any knowledge of a woman named Newby with a baby, perhaps because she had not joined the train at the Gare de Lyon but had been shunted round the Ceinture in the Istanbul coach. He also refused to take delivery of the basket. In a last desperate attempt to hand it over, Alphonse approached the Stationmaster and begged the use of his public address system. The Stationmaster, like the *Chef de Train*, was a bureaucratic monster. He refused permission for this, and also the request to hold the train for a few minutes while Alphonse went through the sleeping cars, with the words, 'It is in this way, at the moment of departure of a great train, that accidents can occur if orders are reversed.' And the train left without the basket. All this I learned from Bill, my moustachioed friend, the following morning. The news plunged me into unspeakable gloom.

Three days later I received a letter from Wanda, postmarked Domodossola, at the Italian end of the Simplon Tunnel.

'I am glad I was able to send a telegram telling you not to send the basket,' she wrote. 'You remember that silver we bought for Valeria?'

(Valeria was Wanda's greatest friend. She lived in Fontanellato and was getting married shortly. We had bought her six place settings of cutlery from George Jensen in Bond Street, the most expensive wedding present we ever bought anybody before or since.) 'This seemed a good time to take it to her,' she continued, 'and because of the Customs I put it in the basket under the food. It will have to wait now until next year. There was no need to worry about Sonia. Everyone was very kind. The cook on the ship cooked just the right food for her and let me into his kitchen to see for myself, and on the train from the Gare de Lyon the chef in the *ristorante* made purée with lots of fresh vegetables. He even had spinach. In a couple of hours we shall be in Milano and there the controllers of our *vagone* is going to get me more fresh food, which will also be cooked for me.'

A week or so later Bill, the man with the moustache, telephoned to say that someone on the French side of the Channel with a horrible sense of humour had returned the basket to him full of what was now putrescent baby food.

'I don't suppose you want it,' he said. 'It means you're coming all the way here and going through Customs, all for a few nappies and feeding bottles.'

I told him about the silver. There was nothing else to do in the circumstances, and there was just a faint hope that it might be still there.

'Half a mo,' he said. 'I'll just take it outside and turn it out on the concrete.'

Soon he was back. 'Sorry,' he said. 'You're having a run of bad luck. There's nothing but a nasty smell.

'I expect it was Alphonse,' he went on. 'I told you he was in the Resistance. He might be soft-hearted about babies but not about anything else.'

Days and Nights on
the Orient Express

———————— ·❖· ————————

LONG BEFORE I acquired employers well enough off to enable us to travel in a wagon-lit if we wanted to do so, which was when I became a fashion buyer in the early sixties, the real Orient Express had ceased to be a practicable means of getting to Istanbul.

The only sensible way of getting to Istanbul by train was on the Simplon-Orient, later named the Direct Orient Express, from the Gare de Lyon. The Direct Orient finally ceased to run in May 1977, by which time it was infested with *malviventi* who drugged and robbed the passengers and subjected them to even worse indignities, which was the end of it.

In order to join the Simplon-Orient, or the Direct Orient, from London, you took the boat train from Victoria to Dover. A more chic way was to board the Golden Arrow All-Pullman train at Victoria and the equally luxe Flêche d'Or on the other side of the Channel. This just gave time for anyone of an adventurous disposition to take a taxi from the Gare du Nord to the Gare de Lyon, stopping off at the Ritz Bar in rue Cambon on the way. Otherwise you could stay on the train and be trundled round Paris with your luggage, as Wanda had been, on the Ceinture to the Gare de Lyon. The scenes on the platform of the Gare de Lyon, for anyone interested in such trivia, and most people are, were in their way memorable. In those now far-off days the travelling rich could actually be seen travelling: on trains, transatlantic liners, even in aeroplanes – how they contrive to move about now is a mystery – and at the Gare de Lyon the platform was crowded with conspicuous consumers. Very few of these conspicuous consumers on the Simplon or the Direct Orient held sleeping-car tickets for the through carriage to Istanbul by way of Bulgaria. The majority boarded cars bound for Milan, Rome, Naples, Venice, Thessalonica or Athens, which could be detached from whichever of these two expresses they were part of along the line and, if necessary, attached to other expresses on other lines.

Wearing heavy overcoats (let no one tell you that it isn't cold in Istanbul in winter), armed with passports stamped with hard-to-get Yugoslav and Bulgarian transit visas, without which the journey could not be made, we walked up the platform at the Gare de Lyon past the big blue sleeping cars with the bronze ciphers of the Compagnie Internationale des Wagons-Lits et des Grand Expresses Européens embossed on their sides until we reached a *voiture-lits* with the magic words PARIS–LAUSANNE – MILAN – VENEZIA – BEOGRAD – SOFIA –ISTANBUL displayed on it in black letters on a white ground.

There, with the words of the wagons-lits *conducteur* ringing in their ears, '*En voiture, s'il vous plâit, Madame, M'sieur!*', we set our feet on the portable mounting block which he had placed there for the convenience of his passengers and hoisted ourselves up the two tall steps to the interior.

Once inside the wagon, having distributed largesse to the porters who had unceremoniously shoved our heavy leather luggage through an open window, and to the *conducteur* in anticipation of further rewards, we were able to take a brief look at the compartment that was to be our home for at least the next 48 hours and 3,041 kilometres.

We admired the wealth of inlaid mahogany, the shining brasswork, the glittering mirrors, the water carafes, heavy enough to lay out the most thick-skulled train robber, the white linen drugget on the floor, the spotless bed linen and towels which would become progressively less so as the journey unfolded, the little hook on the bulkhead beside one's bunk to hold a man's pocket watch in a world in which almost everyone now possessed a wrist watch. We were also pleased at the thought, although we did not actually inspect it, of the chamber pot hidden away like a bomb in its special receptacle which when sufficiently filled enabled it to be up-ended and its contents deposited on the permanent way below, which was less hazardous than attempting to throw it out of the window in the Simplon Tunnel.

Then after whoever was driving the thing had caused it to give its habitual, shattering premonitory lurch in anticipation of the actual departure, we were off.

Because we were hungry we set off immediately for the dining car, in anticipation of the announcement of the *premier service*, as the train clonked out through the 12ème *arrondissement*, past the Entrepôts de Bercy, the great warehouses on the left bank of the Seine – now no more, as no more as the Simplon-Orient Express. The cutlery and the glasses tinkled on the snowy tablecloths, which even before the train left the station had begun to be speckled with tiny flecks of soot from the coal-burning engine.

And while we drank our aperitifs we studied the interesting menu which had the name of the *chef de brigade* and his team inscribed on it, while the train, gathering speed now, passed through Maisons Alfort and Villeneuve-St Georges, where Balzac's widow once resided, places we would be unlikely to visit then or ever.

Then to bed with a little violet light burning high up in the roof of the *coupé*, as the train roared down the line towards Dijon, only to be woken at some ghastly hour to find it at a standstill, 462 kilometres from Paris, at Vallorbe, a station on the edge of the strange no man's land between France and Switzerland, with a man plodding past groaning 'Vallorbe! . . . Vallorbe!' Here the train erupted with Swiss guards and customs men, all full of fight, who were content to look at the passports which the *conducteurs* held for their inspection in neat piles without harassing the wagons-lits passengers, saving their energies for those they would harass in the lower-class carriages.

Breakfast was coffee and fresh croissants – put aboard the train at Lausanne and eaten as it snaked along the shores of Lake Geneva in the grey early morning. Then up the valley of the Rhône, still in dark shadow, to Brig, where the Finsteraarhorn and the Jungfrau loomed over us, and then into the Simplon Tunnel to run 12½ miles under the Lepontine Alps, with the little violet light burning in the *coupé*. Then, out into the golden winter sunshine of Italy.

On Lake Maggiore the cork and cedar trees and the oleanders rose above the early mist that enshrouded the Borromean Islands.

At Milan there was plenty of time to buy a *Corriere* and stock up with Chianti, *prosciutto di Parma*, *salame di Felino*, black olives and the white bread called *pane di pasta dura*, for whatever periods of enforced abstinence awaited us in the Balkans.

Here, too, at Milan, a restaurant car was attached, in which you could eat delicious *pasta al forno* and drink Barbera, while the train drove on through the *pianura*, the great plain of Northern Italy. Then, some four hours outward-bound from Milan, we rumbled through the hideous environs of Mestre and out along the causeway to the beautiful, dying city in the Lagoon, which there was no time to visit.

After Venice we crossed rivers that in the First World War had literally run with blood – the Piave, the Tagliamento and the Isonzo.

After Trieste there was the Yugoslav Customs with rather smelly officials rooting in our luggage before the train climbed into the great limestone wilderness of the Carso, 1,200 feet above the sea; and from there it ran down through the Javornik Range, the densely wooded Slovenian mountains in which wolves and bears still lived. No more restaurant cars on the Direct-Orient after Trieste until we reached Turkey – we were glad of the food and drink we had bought at Milan Station. The *conducteur* brewed us tea and coffee. Things were better ordered on the Simplon-Orient – at least there was a Yugoslav dining car as far as Belgrade.

After Ljubljana, the train ran down the valley of the Sava to Belgrade behind a big steam engine that howled as it went, as if to express its feelings about the human condition. From now on it was steam all the way and it was difficult to sleep and everything became grubbier and grubbier. We spent hours talking with the *conducteur* of our wagon, who was from La Villette, behind the Gare de L'Est, and could by now have done with a shave.

He told us stories about such *eminences grises* as Gulbenkian père and Zaharoff, the armaments king, both of whom commuted on these trains; tales of the express being snowed up and attacked by bandits in Thrace; and girls being put on, and later taken off, the train. It was very cold now and he spent much time stoking the coal-burning stove in what was now, after Belgrade, the sole remaining wagon-lit on the train. Whenever the train stopped at a station, it was besieged by country people carrying huge, crumbling paper parcels in lieu of luggage. In the fields we saw men and women clustered around fires, wearing thick waistcoats and tall fur hats.

At Nis, 2,216 kilometres from Paris, the guide book said that there was a tower constructed with Serbian skulls by a Serbian despot in 1808, but it was invisible from the railway, and when we finally contrived to visit it years later, rather disappointing. At Dimitograd Bulgarian Customs officials were more friendly, less prying than the Yugoslavs. Perhaps they were too cold to care. Here, a huge steam locomotive was attached to the train which panted up with it through a rocky defile and in thick snow to the Dragoman Pass.

We were beginning to be hungry now. Our Italian food was finished and we had no Bulgarian leva to buy anything with: huge queues at the stations made money-changing impossible.

After Sofia lay the wildest country of the entire route, on the borders of Turkey, Bulgaria and Greece. Then, from Edirne (in Turkey further great difficulties with money) with a Turkish dining car attached at last, across the windswept, snowy plains of Eastern Thrace, past Çorlu, where the train was snowed up in 1929, and down to the Sea of Marmara. Then round the seaward walls of Istanbul and out to Seraglio Point, where the Sultan used to have his unwanted odalisques drowned in weighted sacks, and into the Sirkeci Station 3,041 kilometres from the Gare de Lyon.

Under the Crust of Coober Pedy

In 1971 Wanda and I flew to Coober Pedy in the Stuart Range, in South Australia, the location of the world's biggest opal field.

As we came in to land, Coober Pedy and its environs looked like Verdun after five months under artillery fire; what appeared to be shell holes were shafts of workings which went down 20 feet or so beneath the surface, into the desert sandstone in which the opals lurk and are found, or not, according to the skill and luck of the miners. Other holes in the earth's crust, not distinguishable at this height, were the chimney and air inlets of the underground houses in which the majority of the permanent inhabitants lived troglodytic lives, having dug their multi-roomed residences out of the sandstone and equipped them with every imaginable and unimaginable convenience (one of the more unimaginable being a revolving bed surrounded by mirrors, whose owner, a half-French, half-Hungarian gentleman, proudly demonstrated it to me).

The remaining unfortunates, who included the majority of the Aborigines, lived on the surface in the unimaginable horror of corrugated-iron huts or else in caravans, some of which were equipped with air-conditioning. Unimaginably horrible because in summer here the temperature rises to a shattering 140°F, shade temperatures reach the high 120s, and life is only tolerable underground, where the temperature never rises much above 80°F – less with air-conditioning. In winter the temperature outside sinks to the low 40s – the lowest ever recorded was 26°. Coober Pedy is a rugged place.

There was no surface water in the town. What water there was, which was very salty, was pumped from 350 feet underground into a solar still. The inhabitants were rationed to 25 gallons a week, not that many of them actually drank water. Until 1966 it was carted all the way from Mathesson's Bore, 80 miles to the north.

There was not a lot to see on the surface of Coober Pedy (even the pretty little Roman Catholic church, which was like a catacomb, was underground) once we had seen the excellent hospital, the motels, the two or three eating places, played cricket on the cricket pitch, and had drinks in the Italian club to which we had been lucky enough to get an introduction. Even the buildings on either side of the dirt road which was the main street only had a skyline at dawn and at dusk. In the evening the great clouds of dust thrown up by the trucks and cars whirling into town against the sunset were a marvellous sight. By that time many of the Aborigines who spent their days scratching for opals among the spoil of abandoned diggings, the half-castes and the completely decayed white men, were all lying semi-comatose against a fence surrounded by empty port bottles.

There were few Australians born and bred among the miners. Almost all of them were Europeans who emigrated to this distant land because they found life intolerable in their own – Slovenes, Serbo-Croats, Italians, Greeks, East Germans, Poles, Czechs, Spaniards, all dreaming of the day when they would make a strike and take the next plane out.

Anyone could become an opal miner. No experience was necessary. All you needed were lots of guts, a partner you could trust when he was down the mine alone with the opals, and a Miner's Right which you could buy for 50 cents at the Post Office. It entitled you to prospect a claim 50 yards by 50 for a month, after which, if you wanted to continue working it, you had to register your claim at a cost of under Aus$10 a year. You also needed a pick, shovel, hand auger, carbide light, windlass and ladders.

Professional opal buyers came here from all over the world. The miners would accept nothing for their opals but cash; not even travellers cheques would do. And they gave no receipts for fear of being identified by the Inland Revenue. All buyers were forced to have large quantities of cash about their person. Most buyers were therefore armed, but in spite of this some buyers still disappeared.

Digging started at dawn and soon after noon most miners had had enough. Then the long bar in the Opal Motel (men only) filled up and stayed full until about 10 p.m., by which time Slovenes, Poles, Irishmen, Czechs and even an occasional Englishman were either slithering to the floor or else collapsing as if pole-axed, according to their powers of resistance. During this time, ten hours or so, nothing had been discussed except opals, not even women.

This was a tough town which all through the hot months was almost entirely without women. The girls came to Coober Pedy at the beginning of autumn, around the first of June, as regularly as migrant swallows. They came in air-conditioned coaches and the first arrivals were met at the bus stop and straight away carried bodily underground. They cleaned up a packet. One wonders what would happen if an outing of lady school teachers arrived at the same time.

We quitted this amazing place with real regret and flew on eastwards over Lake Torrens, a ghastly, ghostly, dazzlingly white saline expanse, to Hawker, a pleasant little nineteenth-century town, in the middle of what used to be vast wheat fields, now sheep country, in the Flinders Ranges. Here I met Jeff Findley, who had been asked to take me into Outback country.

'The Nips have got the six-cylinder Land Rovers licked with their Toyotas,' he said gloomily. 'If I was Lord Stokes I'd be real worried.' I wrote to Lord Stokes pointing this out, but he was so unworried that he didn't bother to reply.

We drove up through the Ranges by way of the Hills of Arkaba, where there was a sheep station but scarcely any sheep, which was not surprising considering that in this sort of country at this time of year there were probably only 10,000 sheep to 10,000 acres.

Finally, we arrived at the Parachilna Hotel, 57 miles from Hawker, but longer by the route we took, just at the moment when the sky fell in and this particular part of the Outback and a good 500 miles north of it were deluged with water.

It is almost as difficult in retrospect to remember this night at the Parachilna Hotel as it is to forget it. Difficult either way with the malt whisky flowing like beer and the beer like spring water, and Angus Donald McKenzie, the proprietor of this old and extensive hotel, playing a lament on the bagpipes, with the rain falling so thick outside that it was difficult to breathe and while all that was going on trying to listen to old Bert Rickaby, who was eighty or ninety, I forget which, but looked sixty, who the previous week had opened up his stomach with a pen knife and got out 26 ounces of fluid, presumably pure Glen Grant.

'. . . so I got some salt,' Rickaby was speaking about some more ancient affliction now, 'cut the poisoned part three times on top and twice underneath, rubbed in salt from the lake, and then went into Maree and got piss drunk.'

The rain ended any serious attempt to reach the real uninhabited Outback. Having charged through Beltana, a ghost town deep in mud, population six families – three Aboriginal, three white – and water-courses which engulfed the transfer box on our Range Rover, all the next day we sat on the bank of Emu Creek waiting for it to subside while the mile-long trains of freight cars on the Central Australian Railway, from Alice Springs, hummed down the line triumphantly above us.

The magnificent Victorian hotels we came across might have been in the West Country. They had hitching rails outside which were not for horses any more, but had been reinforced to prevent the owners of Nissans and Toyota Land Cruisers, all fitted with winches, lifting hooks and kangaroo bars, from driving them through the retaining wall of the hotel and into the bar inside.

So far as I could make out most of the fighting in Outback pubs was on account of somebody refusing to have a beer with someone else.

'Eric, meet Ron, John, Les, Stan, Alan, Willie, Jimmy. This is Eric from England. How about a beer, Eric?'

I stood in the wide main street outside the Birdsville Hotel in south-west Queensland, which was the epitome of all the Outback pubs I had seen, watching the sun race up behind the trees out of the Diamantina River, which was often nothing but a series of dry furrows.

The rain had accomplished what seemed almost impossible in country where the last drops of the stuff worth measuring fell four years before, a whole foot of it coming down in a single night early in March the previous year, and that was only the beginning. Since then Birdsville and its eighty-odd inhabitants had been cut off by flooding from the outside world except by air.

I had seen many interesting things during my travels round Australia. I had been to the East Alligator River on the edge of Arnhem Land, which had large and horrid estuarine crocodiles at its mouth and fresh-water ones with red eyes further up. I had seen swarms of magpie geese, spoonbills, ibis and variously coloured cockatoos and lotus birds with giant feet which helped them to skid over the surface of the water lily pads, red wallaroos and wild horses up to their flanks in water, and wild Indian buffaloes with 10- and 11-foot spreads of horn.

I had been to Arkaroola in the northern Flinders Ranges on a road that was like an old-fashioned, dark red blancmange and seen the uranium mountains that were so difficult to reach that they had to use camels to get the stuff out for the Manhattan Project in 1943 and 1944, and had stayed in their shadow in a brand new motel.

I had flown hundreds and hundreds of miles, over the coal mines at Leigh Creek and the dingo fence which stretches right across South Australia from New South Wales to the west, and I had just missed being bitten by a deadly spider in the meat house of an abandoned homestead at Tea Creek, and now I just wanted to sit down quietly and think about the Outback without seeing any more of it because, quite suddenly, it had become a little too much for me.

Walking the Plank

'YOU HAVE RATHER walked the plank, haven't you, Eric?' Donald Trelford, then Deputy Editor of the *Observer*, said when he heard that I had decided to leave the paper and become a freelance writer. For almost ten years, from 1963 to 1973, I had been its Travel Editor, one of the few jobs in my life from which I had not been sacked and had really enjoyed.

But I was not as worried about the prospect of walking the plank as I probably should have been. I knew all about walking planks and what happened to the good guys who did so. I still remembered, back in the twenties, seeing Douglas Fairbanks Senior, suffering this fate in a film, *The Black Pirate*. He had been shoved off the end of one swathed in chains to the accompaniment of some frenetic work on the piano by a pianist who was located where the orchestra would have been if it had been a theatre (sometimes he would be accompanied by a drummer to simulate the sounds of gunfire). At that time all films were silent ones.

But in spite of this, now fathoms deep in the Caribbean Sea, and with apparently inexhaustible reserves of oxygen in his lungs, Fairbanks had been able to rid himself of his chains; and then, having swum under the keel, had clambered aboard the enemy vessel, found to hand a swivel gun loaded with grape shot, with which he swept the decks of the murderous scum who had tried to do him in. (At least this is how I remember it years later.)

He was a corker, Douglas Fairbanks Senior, was, and he could fill a cinema such as the Broadway in Hammersmith, or the Blue Halls, over the river from where I lived in Barnes – both of which smelt strongly of disinfectant – with just the suspicion of a twirl of one of his elegant moustaches. I think he had moustaches. All this happened long before Donald Trelford was even thought of.

That year of my departure from the *Observer*, 1973, the year I walked the plank, was one in which, all of a sudden, everything started happening that was needed – to continue the gangplank metaphor – to keep me and the rest of our family afloat.

It was the year I was commissioned to write a history of exploration* for what seemed at that time a gigantic fee of £12,000, with the condition that the book had to be delivered in six months and that no royalties would be paid until 125,000 copies had been sold. A prodigious number for a book with a selling price at that time of £10.50. Sales actually came close to this figure, but then, mysteriously, stopped.

At the same time I was asked to become the principal figure in a BBC film, one of a series entitled *One Pair of Eyes*, the intention of which, I was told, was to find out what made me tick.

As if all this was not enough to contend with, Wanda decided that this was an appropriate moment to sell our house in Wimbledon, which meant that until we bought another one, so far as Britain was concerned, we would be homeless.

The house, a pretty, early-Victorian one, was hidden away in a cul-de-sac called Sunnyside on the slopes of Wimbledon Hill, and she had surprisingly little difficulty in selling it. There were two contenders, but only one of them was seriously interested. The eventual buyer was at that time a professional circus clown. It was Wimbledon Week when he came to see it and the spiraea was in full flower. The garden looked wonderful.

Suddenly, for the first time in our joint lives, we enjoyed the sensation of being quite well off. We extinguished our overdraft and, bubbling with euphoria, left the Midland Bank which had made our life a misery for so many years, to carry on without us.

The house was crammed from top to bottom with all the loot and junk accumulated in more than twenty years of travel: primitive paintings, among them some from Haiti, Ethiopia, Bali, the shores of the Mediterranean and the Côte d'Ivoire. One of them, a spirited impression of the Turkish city of Bursa, in the manner of Osbert Lancaster, was painted in 1902 on a piece of linoleum. There was also a fine Aboriginal painting on bark, from Van Diemen's Land, of an emu.

---

* *The World Atlas of Exploration*, Mitchell Beazley, 1975.

And there were *kilims*, flat weave rugs made by the Yürük nomads during their wanderings on and off the high Anatolian plateau, with which they used to cover the floors of their tents.

And there was the entire Ordnance Survey of Great Britain at one inch to the mile, all 189 sheets of it mounted on canvas. And about 2,000 books, including dozens of Murray and Baedeker guides; and the entire *Observer Colour Magazine* from its inception in 1963; and all the manuscripts of my books that I should have thrown away but hadn't; and a complete set of the 1879 edition of the *Encyclopaedia Britannica*, in a demountable bookcase (useful if one needed to consult it in the wilderness while on yak's back, all thirty-five volumes of it).

And there were bellows cameras with shutters that made a noise like the Traitor's Gate being slammed shut when they were fired off; and there were models of the sort of ships and boats I had sailed or rowed in – a *curragh* from the Arran Islands, *oolaks* and *panswais* from the Ganges, a four-masted Cape Horn sailing ship, a *caïque* from Ruad, the Syrian island in the Eastern Mediterranean on which they are still built to this day.

There was a large, empty tin of what had contained a kilo of Malossol caviar – the two halves of the tin held together by what looked like the inner tube of a car tyre – which I had brought from Leningrad to Moscow on New Year's Day 1965, and from Moscow to the Hook of Holland stuck on the front of a succession of steam engines in order to stop it going off in what were tropically heated carriages.

And there was a black felt suit with matching double-breasted waistcoat, so thick that it could stand up without anyone in it. It had been made for me by a Bulgarian tailor who had his premises in one of the sinister, labyrinthine lanes between what was then the Old Fishmarket by the Galata Bridge in Istanbul – a suit I never wore.

And there were cricket bats steeped in linseed oil which I hadn't used for so many years that I had forgotten how to play the game; and a pair of sculls belonging to my father that I couldn't bring myself to get rid of; and a couple of pairs of cross-country running shoes fitted with spikes which I didn't think I was going to need while writing a history of discovery, and a pair of cycling shoes. And there were *jellabs* brought back from North Africa, long garments made from thick, creamy wool; and lots of straw hats in various stages of collapse – one of them of a sort that Galician women wore on their heads, which were sufficiently robust to support a basket with some 60lb of fish in it; and there were a couple of navy blue cotton suits of the sort that were currently being worn by something like a billion Chinese; and there was a dustbin full of sandals – mostly, for some inscrutable reason, left-footed – which we planned to leave at the Wimbledon rubbish tip.

And there were Chinese hats with ear-flaps; and a brand-new Romanian railway guard's navy blue wool coat with an imitation fur collar and entirely lined with sheepskin, bought brand-new from a state pawnshop in Bucharest for around £12; and there were mowing machines and a garden roller and Primus stoves and Bergan rucksacks and bicycles and what were known as Itisa tents made from the finest imaginable cotton back in 1935 and still usable in 1996,* and real eiderdown sleeping bags which cost a small fortune; and walking sticks, one of which concealed within it a sword and another a cosh, which my father commissioned from Brigg, the umbrella and stick maker in Piccadilly, when he had to travel in 'foreign parts'. And there were fifteen years of back numbers of *Vogue* and *Harper's*, *aide mémoires* to my life and times in the rag trade. And there was an enormous hammock made by ladies working in the gaol in Merida in Yucatan which could swallow up a family of five with ease. And thousands of prints without negatives and negatives without prints, and transparencies, some of which were already beginning to fade.

These were just a few of the things, *objets retrouvés*, which had swum before our eyes while the very old-fashioned-looking removal men – all of them wearing green baize aprons and themselves smelling of a mixture of, could it be linseed and old furniture? – removed and wrapped them up in old yellowing newspapers (that I would not have been surprised to learn had the date 4 August 1914 on them) before stowing them away in one of a large number of plywood tea chests with *Army and Navy Stores* stencilled on them in black.

The removal men had almost completed this packing-up process and had already begun to load into the van some of the chests from the upper parts of the house, comporting themselves with a stately slowness, when the director of the film in which we were to take part arrived on

---

* Made by Camtors (Camp and Sports Co-operators).

the scene and asked us to tell the removal men to bring all the containers back into the house as he wanted to film the process of the Newbys packing up and leaving for pastures new.

Mischa Scorer, who was responsible for this decision, was young, brilliant, charming and, as he now proved himself to be, utterly ruthless. What eventually resulted was a rather funny piece of *cinéma vérité*, based on there being nothing more likely to drive anyone to suicide than unpacking a whole lot of old tea chests, filled to the brim with things you will probably never need again, and then repacking them.

It was Mischa who told me that I would need my spiked cross-country shoes for a sequence in which I was to run across Wimbledon Common and Richmond Park, something I used to do quite often, mostly in winter just before dusk when they were wild and lonely places. I did this to let off steam and to think about what I was going to write next and how I was going to approach the subject. This was years before jogging became a worldwide pastime.

He also told me I would need my cycling shoes for the cycling scenes and they eventually turned up at the bottom of another box. I take size 12s in shoes and my bike had narrow, racing pedals, so there was no question of just walking into a shop and finding a pair – mine had to be made-to-measure. Both items were at the bottom of their respective tea chests.

After carousing in the mud on Wimbledon Common and less muddily in Richmond Park – both running events – the whole show was moved to Marble Arch. Here, if the venue seemed to Mischa to be sufficiently hazardous, I was to be filmed riding round and round it on my twelve-speed touring bicycle which had dropped handlebars. This, too, was long before mountain bikes with triple chainwheels and eighteen or twenty-one gears appeared on the scene.

After seemingly endless circumnavigations, eventually the filming took place with me wired for sound and the crew filming me from the back of a van as I pedalled towards them at about 15mph, at the same time gibbering into the microphone in an attempt to express my feelings about riding round the Marble Arch. The effect of a solitary cyclist talking away to himself, in fact shouting away to himself – the only way I could make myself heard above the roar of the traffic as I crossed and recrossed its bows – must have given other road users the impression that they were in the presence of a lunatic, which in effect I was. It was only when I saw some film of me and my bike taken through a lens which caused everything behind me in the way of traffic to loom precipitously overhead that I realized how dangerous it was.

Follies, Holy Wells, Great Cliffs and Storms were other subjects I had told Mischa I would be interested in elaborating on in *One Pair of Eyes*. All these were to be found in abundance on the West Coast of Ireland anywhere between Malin and Mizen Head. But storms, even in winter, were difficult to predict. At one moment we found ourselves standing by to fly to South Africa where a big storm was threatening to take place; but then a whole series of them, mostly force 9 and 10, began to blow up on the Loop Head Peninsula at the mouth of the Shannon in County Clare, which were stormy enough for anything a sane person would want to be involved in.

It was at this time, with a force 10 gale raging and very much against my inclination, that Mischa told me to traverse a large, inclined ledge of rock that was being swept by big seas and it was here, while I was standing on the edge, wondering whether to go through with it, that one of the waves picked me up and threw me down with such violence that a doctor had to be summoned to give me a shot of morphia. Meanwhile, Mischa carried on filming without giving me the opportunity to change out of my wet clothes. Working with Mischa could be a health hazard. I should have sued him.

When the excitement of being asked to write a history of exploration had to some extent abated and I was actually confronted with the necessity of getting on with it, I felt like Hillary and Tenzing must have felt at the foot of that Everest. What I soon realized was that I knew far less about the subject than my new employers thought I knew. They had already assembled a team of researchers of mature student age whose job it was, ostensibly, to help me in the search for material; but some of these had already been commandeered to do research on the pictorial content of the book, for which it grew ever more apparent the actual text had a more or less supporting role.

At first I decided to make a list of all the well and not so well known explorers, beginning with the Ancient World, and I eventually ended up with a lot of notebooks crammed with unhelpful entries, such as:

'Egypt – Old Kingdom – Papyrus in the reign of Sneferu (4th dynasty c. 2613–3494). Records imaginary voyage and shipwreck – Cary and Warmington, The Ancient Explorers, p. 233 and 239. See note on Celinis-chef, Sur un ancien conte Egyptien, 1881, p. 4–8, and in Maspero.' And so on until I felt my reason going.

In fact, mercifully for me, it soon turned out that there was not going to be enough time to do it in this way, or even decide what was to go in and what was to be thrown out. By now we had taken temporary refuge in the ground floor flat of some great friends of ours in Spencer Park, Wandsworth, and no sooner had we moved in than great piles of books and *aide mémoires* began to arrive on the premises. They were either brought by special messengers on motor cycles or in taxis from the publishers' premises off the Charing Cross Road. Then, having found the books I needed, many of which had come from the London Library (and a lot from the Wandsworth Public Library, which had enormous numbers of travel books in its vaults), and having, for example, identified those which dealt with the Portuguese voyages to Africa and the East in the fifteenth and sixteenth centuries, I opened them at page one and began to go through them and sometimes even began to write about them, without, usually, having the slightest idea what would eventually happen. Suddenly, the whole world began to spread out before me. It was all rather exciting.

Having done this, I used to send my typescript back to the publishers where the editors would mangle and rewrite it in their own, inimitable fashion. But I could scarcely complain. They had no choice. All my contributions were over-written by many thousand words. I had, and still have, the conviction that I must let the reader know if I discover anything interesting, and unfortunately so many things are interesting. At least they are to me.

Apart from a month in Italy, where I took on the Arctic and Antarctica in a temperature of 90°F, my daily programme was unchanging. I used to get up at dawn and run 2½ miles round Spencer Park, a beautiful, Arcadian place surrounded by noble trees, before returning for a good breakfast, produced by Wanda, who had been making the bed – unless she made the bed we couldn't get into the room. Lunch was a sandwich. I then worked all through the afternoon until dusk, then ran another 2½ miles.

Meanwhile every day Wanda set off, pedalling a bicycle, for the house we had bought in Kennington, which she was refurbishing. Before dinner I had a large whisky and with dinner shared a bottle of wine with Wanda. Then we both went to bed, whacked. We didn't have a television.

This kind of existence went on for five months, by which time I began to feel like the Beast of Glamis, or the Man in the Iron Mask. Now, more than twenty-five years later, I am awed by my industry and enthusiasm for what was a rather difficult task.

Follies and Grottoes

In 1974 we bought Pear Tree Court, a house on the banks of the Harbourne River at Harbertonford between Totnes and Kingsbridge, in South Devon. It was a pretty, Gothic house, its principal disadvantage being that it was so far from London (about 200 miles) that we practically had to bribe our friends to come for the weekend. It also had a rather forbidding wall surrounding it which gave the impression that it was just about to fall on us, quaking away below, but it never did.

Having acquired a Gothic house, our thoughts turned to a Gothic grotto. The nearest grotto to Pear Tree Court – whether it was Gothic or not was conjectural – was in what had been the park of Oldstones, a burnt-out Palladian house near Blackawton, the property of the Cholwich family, in which there were said to be two grottoes.

The approach was by a path which led from the house through an avenue of trees to what was on this particular day a distinctly gloomy valley with three small, artificial lakes in it – nearby there was a grotto in poor condition.

Beyond the valley there was a wood, and at its far end, in a cold and extremely exposed position, a granite plaque was set in a stone wall and inscribed with the following:

> Within a Wood unknown to Public View
> From Youth to Age a Reverend Hermit grew
> The Moss his Bed, the Cave His Humble Cell,
> His Food the Fruits, his drink the Crystal Well.
> Remote from Man with God he passed His Days,
> Pray'r all his Business, all his Pleasure Praise.

And in the wood, at the end of a cutting, there was, it was said, the cave in which a resident hermit, the most rare of beings in such an inhospitable climate as that of Britain, spent many years holed up in order to gratify his patron, and without catching his death of cold.

We never found this second grotto. I told Wanda that the grotto by the lake was not the sort of grotto I wanted, anyway. What I wanted was a more dotty grotto. It was almost the shortest, certainly the coldest day of the year and Wanda was sufficiently depressed to the point of not wanting a grotto at all.

'Let's go home,' she said. We did so and I promptly went down with what was called flu, but was really nothing more than over-exposure to the elements. A short time later, when I came downstairs to begin a convalescent Christmas, it was Wanda who advanced the idea of building a dotty grotto, as if it had been her idea in the first place.

Eventually, we decided to build a grotto that would also act as a garden shed – planning permission not being necessary at that time for garden sheds less than 12ft high, providing they had ridge roofs, 10ft with any other sort of roof. As a further insurance against the dead hand of the planner, which is inevitably set against follies, except those of their own creation, we were fortunate in being able to site it behind part of the high stone wall which would conceal it from the public eye. It would also enable us to have access to water, without which no grotto is complete, as the River Harbourne flowed conveniently close on the other side of this wall.

The first serious discussion about it took place in the kitchen of the house the following autumn.

2 November.
Beautiful limpid, cloudless morning after a slight night frost. About 10.30 Mr Perring, Wanda and I sat down in the kitchen and went through the Folly Book (*Follies and Grottoes* by Barbara Jones, Constable, £10, an essential work for anyone foolish enough to go into the folly/grotto business).

We are looking for a grotto I *thought* I saw in Barbara Jones's book. It was Gothic, small and built of rough, uncut stones with finials sprouting from the pediment. I must have seen it in *Country Life*, of which I appear to have 5,000 copies in the barn. The one we eventually sketch out for ourselves on the back of an envelope is based on a dramatically scaled down version of part of the entrance to the Hell Fire Caves at West Wycombe in Buckinghamshire, which in its original form would necessitate the introduction of slave labour in order to get it on the go.

Mr Perring of course immediately understands the sort of thing we have in mind. He is attracted by the great gaping entrances to the Hell Fire Caves with blackness behind, like the way into the lair of the Minotaur; but since our entire folly will only be about 6ft wide, such an entrance would leave no space for niches in the frontage, besides being rather draughty.

Eventually we agreed. Niches inside and out, slate ceiling. All to be filled with shell motifs; a marble head – Neptune, lion, satyr or whatever spouting water into a basin lined with variegated pebbles, from which it runs back into the river. Floored with egg-shaped stones from the beach at Branscombe, between Beer and Seaton. Chesil Bank, a 16-mile long beach of shingle with a clay foundation, between Bridport and the Isle of Portland, is too far away. God knows where we shall find the shells – we shall probably need thousands. Outside, ridge slate roof, masked by pediment with four rough finials to simulate living rock. The whole thing to be 7ft high, 6ft wide with a 3ft door and 7ft deep.

Mr Perring is a retired stonemason. He can do anything with stone except bend it and he knows how to make those huge stone balls that balance on pillars at the gates of the grander sorts of houses and occasionally fall on delivery vans. He is still a demon for work and not unnaturally thinks the country has gone to the dogs; if one accepts his standards of activity it is difficult not to agree with him. His immediate reaction is to mend a thing rather than 'replace the unit'. Consequently he never throws anything away as 'it might come in useful'.

He is also a vegetable gardener of near, if not actual, genius and he has won more cups for his vegetables than anyone else in these parts – there is a Perring Cup to be competed for by the less inspired.

Above all he is a man of natural taste, especially in anything to do with building – the country towns and villages in this part of the world are the results of the labours of generations of such men, now mostly dead and gone.

Mr Perring was chafing to begin and I was dispatched forthwith (from now on my role was no more than that of a drudge) to buy materials – just to be getting on with, and it didn't go far – 5cwt sand, 2 sackfuls shingle, 2 sacks cement and a packet of chalk to mark the outline of the building on the back wall. We already had some dark limestone left over from rebuilding the porch, which would see us through for a bit.

By the end of the second day he/we had the foundations in, reinforced with bed-bars that Mr Perring found in a hedge. 'I told you,' he said. 'Never throw anything away. You never know when it might come in handy.' And then, looking at a sky full of leaden clouds, he added: 'If it rains we'll be *stugged*.'

It didn't and we weren't, and the next day he began to lay the first courses of the walls, breaking the stone as he went. When it began to get dark he knocked off. Before he went home to his tea, prepared by Mrs Perring, he advised me, as it was 5 November, to stuff the letter-box with damp newspaper to prevent the village boys – 'them lot of young toads' – blowing it up with fireworks, also to bar all entrances, which gave us a feeling of being besieged. Thwarted, they blew the lids off two half-filled dustbins, with spectacular results.

6 November.
Fine early, gloomy later. Scour countryside with Mr P for stone suitable for grotto building. Those quarries that have it want £11 a ton and another £10 on top of that to get it home. Our last load of similar stone cost £5 a ton. Late in the afternoon find a worked-out quarry at Ashburton, said to be a thousand years old, which is on the point of closing for ever. £5.50 a ton if we sort it ourselves, so we pick out about 4½ tons by hand with the help of the last quarryman – the others have been made redundant. This quarry is the epitome of melancholy: trees on the cliffs above shedding the last of their leaves down the sheer black walls, defunct machinery, rusty coloured pools of water, the last small heap of usable stones – reminiscent, with a dark, tall-spired church looming over us, of the paintings of Caspar

David Friedrich. The negation of a Jolly Folly; but what a place
to do away with oneself.

7 November.

A lorry arrives in the a.m. and deposits the stone from Ashburton
with such a thunderous noise that neighbours rush into the
street thinking that someone's house has collapsed.

At this time I was trying desperately to write a book, but I soon gave
up. It was obvious that Mr Perring regarded me as being on permanent
call. As soon as I got started writing, I had to wheel more barrow-loads
down to him. One Sunday, in order to snatch a whole day of uninterrup-
ted work – he worked on the grotto Saturdays too – I wheeled down
about fifty barrow loads. On Monday I got it in the neck. 'Don't you
go getting me more than five loads at a time, or I'll be stugged,' he said.
'Any road, a lot of what you brought is a load of old rummage.'

In December we had to go to Istanbul and when we got back on an
evening in Christmas week he had finished his part of it, finials, roof
and all. It was an unforgettable moment, as the three of us stood there
in the darkness illuminating it with a torch. All it needed now was the
pavement, the marble head and the shells.

Like all folly builders we didn't dare to think about how much work
and material had gone into it.

All through that winter, whenever we could find the time, we collected
shells. Weekend guests rash enough to come here for the weekend,
hoping for a quiet Sunday with the newspapers in front of the fire,
found themselves being carried off to freezing, oil-polluted beaches on
which they were forced to work until dusk, bent double, filling rubber
buckets with whelks, clams, many of which had to be rejected because
they were covered in oil, and pretty little pink-flecked shells which
cheered them up momentarily, as they were rather rare. Slapton, the
best of these beaches, was about three miles of shingle and in anything
above force 5 from the east the searchers became invisible at a hundred
yards in a mist of spray.

Even worse was picking up egg-shaped cobbles on the beach at Branscombe. While we were engaged in this task, a man appeared who told
us to clear off. Feeling sure that he was a man of no authority, at least
below low-water mark, and only needing about 300 stones out of some

400 billion still *in situ*, we told him to push off, and he stomped away ostensibly to alert the Police and the National Trust, who own the valley and foreshore; but he must have changed his mind, as we saw him enter his habitation and switch on the telly.

The laying of the pavement to a preconceived design was the most difficult job of all because the floor was slightly assymetrical. In the end we discovered that the only way to do it was to set out the stones on the grass outside and for me to hand them one by one to Wanda, who was working at the face.

By early spring we had what looked like enough shells to reshell the Grotto Room at Woburn. I had brought back a large quantity of pure white whelks, which I had gathered while on a visit to the Pentland Firth; and we had some beautiful single specimens from the Caribbean and the Sulu Sea. With the weather unseasonably warm, I found myself with the loathsome job of cleaning hundreds of great scallop shells, which Wanda had acquired from the floor of a wholesale shell-fish distributor, complete with the original goo inside them which by now had gone off. Wanda designed the shell motifs as she went along, pressing each shell into the special cement mixture devised by Mr Perring. There was not much time for reflection as the cement hardened quickly. Altogether it took her about three and a half days, much less than the 261 days that Catherine, Countess of Tyrone, needed to decorate the grotto at Curraghmore in Waterford in 1754; but the Countess's grotto was more commodious.

In May, while in Italy, we succeeded in running to earth a half-finished marble mask of what we took to be a river god at the Carrara Quarries, and when we had arranged for it to be given more beard and more wrinkles, we brought it home to Harbertonford and Mr Perring set up what he called 'the old gent' in the face of the river wall. That afternoon, for the first and almost the last time that desiccated summer, water gushed from the river god's mouth into the basin below.

The grotto was almost finished. It was everything the three of us hoped it would be, each in our own way: built to last, dotty, cheerful, elegant and – apart from being a place in which spades and forks could be left, although they never have been – completely useless.

To complete it only one thing remained to be set up. A slab recording that I thought of it, Mr Perring built it and Wanda decorated it, together with an appropriate inscription. Mr Perring's remark that dark night when we came back from Istanbul to find the fabric completed will do as well as any: 'If I thought you'd leave here I wouldn't have done it.'

He died before we left Harbertonford. We will never forget him.

Journey through Syria

AT AROUND 7 A.M. on a morning in April 1985 we stumbled across the tracks at the Baghdad Station in Aleppo and there boarded the Taurus Express for onward transportation to Istanbul, some 950 railway miles away to the north-west across the Taurus Mountains and the Anatolian Plateau, and some six days and 3,210 miles, if we went on travelling by train, from Victoria Station.

We were assisted in this embarkation by a kindly Syrian civilian, who helped us to carry our by now rather extensive luggage, which included a large *kilim* rug – kindness which we had found among all classes of the Syrian population, however poor. As no ordinary civilians were allowed on the station unless they were going to travel, he was probably a member of the secret police.

The Express, or parts of it, because such trains have a habit of taking on and shedding rolling stock while en route, sometimes leaving the unwary immured in a siding in an engineless carriage, had recently arrived from Tell Kotchek, a station on the Syrian side of the Syro-Iraqi frontier, 526 miles to the east, which, so far as it was concerned, was now the end of the line. This was because of the Iraqi–Iranian war in which Syria favoured the Iranians.

In more peaceful times it would have started its journey at Baghdad, 660 miles from Aleppo, and would have followed the right bank of the Tigris northwards, passing the ruins of Ashur, the ancient capital of Assyria, founded at the beginning of the third millennium. Ashur was sacked by the Emperor Septimus Severus in AD 198 and completely forgotten until 1903 when a German expedition began to disinter it. It also passed Tikrit, where Saladin, who retook Palestine and Syria from the Crusaders, was born, a city which, after the arrival of Timur Leng and his Mongols on the scene in 1394, also disappeared in similar fashion.

Then, after crossing out of Iraq into Syria at Tell Kotchek, it headed westwards along the Turkish frontier past Jerablus, site of the ancient city of Carchemish on the Euphrates, which T. E. Lawrence helped to excavate on behalf of the British Museum before the First World War, finally rumbling into Aleppo in the early hours of the morning – 15½ hours, if all went well, which it didn't always, outward-bound from Tell Kotchek, 28½ hours from Baghdad. From Aleppo it used to be possible to travel the 249 miles to Beirut by a stopping train; but events in the Middle East had long since fouled up this particular tract of the railway system.

We were no strangers to Syrian trains. We had already travelled from Latakia, the port of Syria opposite Cyprus, to Aleppo in a clean and modern train on a line which winds its way through very rural country close to the Turkish border, south of Antakya, the ancient Antioch.

We had enjoyed this journey but would have enjoyed it a good deal less if we had known that terrorists, said by the Syrians to be Iraqis, had blown its counterpart off the rails the previous week, killing and maiming more than a hundred passengers – the same week that they had blown up a number of country buses, also killing large numbers of people, mostly peasants. It was therefore not surprising that the search we and other passengers had been subjected to at Latakia had been thorough. It is somewhat ironical that it should have been at Latakia, a city widely believed to have housed a training school for terrorists, one of whose old boys is said to have been the man who attempted to kill the Pope. Similar prolonged searches had also taken place before we had been allowed to board the Taurus Express at Aleppo, but to our minds these had not been anywhere near severe enough. We would have expected our *kilim* to have been opened up to find out if there was anything inside it but this never happened.

Altogether we had spent twelve days in Syria, fourteen counting those of arrival and departure, and in the course of them we had seen a lot of what the Syrian Transport and Tourism Marketing Co. (established in 1978 with a capital of 10 million Syrian pounds) can get you to, using their air-conditioned motor coaches, mini-buses and cars, chauffeur-driven. Wild horses wouldn't drag me into a self-drive car in Syria.

A day was sufficient for Damascus, oldest living city in the world, mentioned in the archives of Mari, an even more ancient but long

Departures.

Left Wanda and our daughter, Sonia,
19 Riverview Gardens, Barnes.

Below The Newbys, 1963.

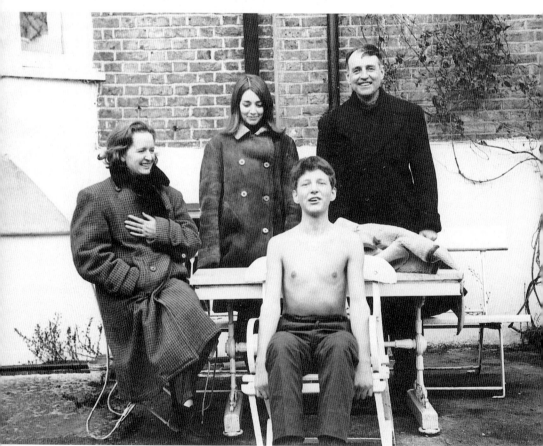

The Orient Express near Çorlu, east of Çerkesköy, where it was snowed up and surrounded by bandits for a week in 1929.

Above Very wet rain falling on me at Parachilna, Australia.

Right and below, Coober Pedy, an opal mining town, Australia.

Above A Gothic folly at Bindon Abbey, Dorset.

Right Wanda among the ruins at Palmyra, described by Dr Thomas Wood as *Tedmor in the Desart*.

Overleaf A great herd of camels in the semi-desert of Northern Rajasthan.

Racing certainties: for the participants, the Palio represents days of plotting to achieve sudden, famous glory.

Bath time: 'Men acquire elephants for prestige reasons, just as a Midland manufacturer might buy a Bugatti or an Isotta Fraschini.'

ruined city on the Syrian Euphrates, as dating back to the twenty-fifth century BC.

A paradise for the Beduin arriving in it from the deserts, Damascus was known variously as the Pearl of the East, the City of Many Pillars, the Necklace of the Throat of Beauty, or as Dimashq Ash-Shem, the Town of Shem, the second son of Noah, from whom descended the Canaanites in whose territory it was. It was also known as the Gate of Mecca because it was from near here in the twelfth month of the Muslim year that the great concourse of pilgrims used to set off for Mecca, taking with it on the back of a dromedary the *mahmal*, the green silk canopy that contained within it a new covering for the Kaaba, the shrine at Mecca.

Constantly fought over, lost and recaptured, twice pillaged by the Mongols, the second time by Timur Leng, who sacked and burnt it, leaving it semi-deserted for some 50 years, today it must be obvious to the most optimistic visitor that he or she has arrived too late to savour what was once its unique beauty. The first city in Syria to benefit from the introduction of cement in 1918, which led to the destruction of so many of its beautiful Arab houses, it is now a veritable hell of automobiles.

How much too late? Fifty years? Steinmatsky's excellent guide book to Syria and Palestine, published in Jerusalem in October 1941, speaks of walking its streets accompanied by the gurgling sounds of running water and breathing its fresh air, 2,200 feet above the sea.

The waters were those of the Barada River, which rises in the Anti-Lebanon mountains, a spur of which, Jebel Kassioun, looms above the city; on its slopes stands the Muslim quarter of Es Salihye. The river runs through the wide valley in which the city stands and from it water was drawn off for the houses, their courtyard gardens, the restaurants and cafés, some of which were supported on piles above the river itself, and for the orchards that hemmed the city in on all sides. Now the Barada flows in a concrete ditch and much of it has been covered.

But all is not lost. At the western end of the old, walled city is the Citadel, built on the site of a Roman camp. From it the great covered Souk el Hamadiye leads to a vast Ommayad mosque, burnt down in 1893 and subsequently rebuilt. Female visitors are admitted providing they don a tent-like black garment, which makes it difficult to identify one's loved one. Close to it are various mausolea which house the tombs of the departed great: that of Saladin, long neglected until refurbished at the Kaiser's expense during his visit to Syria and Palestine in 1898; that of his brother, who built the Citadel; and the mausoleum of Baibars, the Mamluk Sultan of Egypt who was such a formidable opponent of the Crusaders, and that of his son, decorated with a mosaic frieze on a golden ground depicting trees and monuments. And outside the Bab el Saghir, the Little Gate, in the south-western walls, in the cemetery of the same name, are what are said to be the tombs of Fatima and Sayida Sukeina, the daughters of the Prophet, which on Thursdays are watched over by weeping women. And bisecting the walled city from west to east, from a mosque built by Sinan, the greatest of all mosque architects, to the Bab es Charky, a gateway built by the Romans, is the Darb el Mustaqim, the 'Street Called Straight' of the New Testament. Here lived Saul of Tarsus, later St Paul, whose house Ananias visited after Jesus had directed him there in a vision. Much of it, although roofed with corrugated iron, still contrives to look mysterious, almost Piranesian. And at the eastern end, near the gate, are the Christian and what was the Jewish Quarter, both rather muted, the Christian quarter not having ever really recovered from the great massacre of 1860 in which 6,000 Christians were slain. Near the Babes Charky is the Factory of Abou Ahmad in which glass receptacles in beautiful shades of green and blue are blown by men who look as if they have been engaged in this activity for a thousand years. But to me the greatest wonder of Damascus is the Hejaz Railway Station, northern terminus of the narrow-gauge Hejaz Railway, built by Sultan Abdul Hamid with German aid and intended to carry pilgrims all the way to Mecca, 1,120 miles to the south. By 1908 it had reached Medina, 809½ miles from Damascus, but was never completed. Huge stretches of it were subsequently put out of action by Lawrence and the Arabs. Here, surrounded by decrepit but still functioning rolling stock and locomotives with steam up, one has the feeling that the clock stopped somewhere around 1918.

At Maaloula, north of Damascus, a small Christian village hanging on the side of the Anti-Lebanon range, we heard the sounds of Aramaic, the now nearly extinct language spoken by Christ, and drank the most terrible wine in the Byzantine monastery there.

Ninety miles south of Damascus by a road lined with concrete bunkers and a spine-chilling display of Soviet missiles all ready to go, east of Deraa where Lawrence underwent a nasty experience, we saw the great thirty-five-tier Roman theatre, one of the finest in the Middle East, enclosed within the walls of an Arab citadel.

A hundred and fifty miles east of Damascus, out in the stickless sticks that are the Syrian Desert, we stayed at Palmyra. We saw the town first, pale and spooky in the chill dawn, overlooked by a Saracen castle on a rock and the tall sepulchral towers in the valley below, one of them built to contain 399 coffins. In the splendid National Museum in Damascus textiles are preserved which were used in the embalming of the bodies. It was at Palmyra, too, where the caravan routes from Arabia, Persia, India and China met, where linen, wool and silk fabrics were found that appear to have been made in China at the time of the Han dynasty (206 BC to 221 AD). '. . . the greatest quantity of ruins we had ever seen, all of white marble, and beyond them to the Euphrates a flat waste . . .' wrote Dr Robert Wood, down there on a visit in the 1750s, in his magnificent, unportable *Ruins of Palmyra, otherwise Tedmor in the Desart.*

And in the midst of it all the Hotel Zenobie, which must rank as one of the most delightfully eccentric hotels in the Middle East, named after Zenobia, the great queen who conquered Egypt and Asia Minor before being defeated by the Emperor Aurelian, who made her follow his triumphal chariot through the streets of Rome, a dark-haired beauty with black, flashing eyes, the most famous heroine of antiquity.

And some 150 miles north of Damascus, in the mountains high above the Mediterranean, we saw some of the great Crusader castles: Krak des Chevaliers, the most perfectly preserved, besieged by Baibars, capitulated 1271; Markab, built of black basalt on the spur of an extinct volcano, besieged and captured by Qalaun, 1285, after two previous sieges had failed; Sahyun, with a ditch cut through solid rock, between fifty and ninety feet wide and deep, with a slender pinnacle of living rock rising from its depths that supported a drawbridge, besieged and captured by Saladin, 1188.

South of Markab we saw Tartoûs, the port known as Antaradus to the Phoenicians, Constantia to the Byzantines, Tortose to the Crusaders, who built a splendid cathedral there and made it one of their main supply ports. Offshore on the fortified Island of Ruad boats were still being built in much the same way as they were when the Pharaoh Snefru visited it in 3200 BC. On it models of *caïques* are made and for the second time in my life – the first was in 1942 – I bought one.

North-westwards of the Damascus–Aleppo road on a windswept site high above the beautiful valley of the Orontes, full of wild flowers and children peddling antiquities, we saw the Roman/Byzantine ruins of Apamea where Cleopatra stayed while up there visiting Mark Anthony.

West of Apamea, beyond Latakia, an unlovely town, at Ras Shamra, on a mound sixty feet above the sea, the earliest evidences of occupation date to the Neolithic (sixth millennium BC); the latest to the Phoenicians, who occupied it from the sixteenth to the thirteenth century BC, when its brilliant civilization was brought to an end by what the Egyptians knew as the Peoples of the Sea. Among the great treasures found at Ugarit, and now in the National Museum, are a huge ivory panel, decorated with reliefs of various deities, an ivory horn in the shape of an elephant's tusk on which a goddess with a sphinx on each side is shown crossing her hands below her naked breasts, and the head of a king carved in solid ivory and encrusted with gold.

Aleppo, dominated by an enormous Saracenic fortress, was the most interesting city. The most interesting, but not the most luxurious place to stay was the Baron Hotel, built in 1909 on what were then the outskirts of the city, at which time one could shoot wild duck from the front steps. Friendly and idiosyncratic (not for those who demand *any* let alone every modern comfort), it had housed an astonishing variety of guests, among them Lindbergh, Kemal Atatürk, Lady Louis Mountbatten, Dr Schacht, Agatha Christie, Cardinal Spellman, Yuri Gargarin and Mrs Doris Duke, who, if they had all been in residence at the same time, would have created a sensation. While staying there we explored the souks, arguably the most unspoiled and labyrinthine in the Middle East, and bought our *kilim*.

Our last ruin visit in Syria was to Qalaat Semaan, where there was an amazing church north-west of the city. Four basilicas formed a cross as they clustered about the base of a stone cube which had been cut out of the rock; each face measured roughly 15 square feet. Originally 30 feet high, it was on this column and others of various heights that in the pursuit of solitude St Simeon Stylites spent six years, after which he graduated to one 50 feet high, on which he spent a further thirty years, which must have constituted some sort of health hazard to those below.

The next morning the Baron Hotel sent its most trusted man to help us acquire tickets for the Taurus Express which had to be paid for in Syrian pounds and were not available in advance, for the journey to Istanbul.

To us the most memorable part of the ensuing journey on the Taurus Express to Istanbul was seeing the chef in his kitchen washing his hair in one of his larger cooking pots, hair that was very long. Fortunately, in case of emergency, which was what this was, we had equipped ourselves with a supply of food and drink sufficient for a journey a large part of which at that particular time took place in the hours of darkness.

The Palio

IT WAS THE EVENING of 2 July 1987 in the Campo at Siena, the great square shaped like a scallop shell, the heart of what is perhaps the most beautiful medieval city anywhere. Four hundred and twelve murderous steps above it, up in the burnt brick Torre del Mangia, the bell known as Il Sunto tolled while down below endless processions of men and boys went by, all apparently wearing girls' wigs and dressed unseasonally in leather and armour and silks and velvets and hats, some of which looked like jam sponges. (Surely they didn't wear velvet in high summer in Tuscany in the fifteenth century?) They were accompanied by the rolling of drums, the sounding of trumpets and extraordinary displays of flag manipulation which culminated when the virtuosi threw their flags high in the air and caught them in their left hands, failure to catch the flag being one of the innumerable portents of ill omen that attended the celebration of the Palio.

This was the day of the Visitation of the Virgin and the Festa of Our Lady of Provenzano, at whose statue an unspeakable Florentine soldier once took a pot-shot, blowing himself to pieces – serve him right.

It was also the day of the Palio, one of the more hazardous horse races, whose patron she is. It is her likeness which appears on the Palio itself, the long silken banner which is the reward of victory, carried into the Campo on a triumphal car bearing trumpeters and drawn by oxen. A fresh Palio is painted for each successive race and that July she was depicted, together with her Child, floating serenely in a blue heaven while below on earth the astonishing skyline of the city was seen across a Tuscan landscape.

The race was about to begin, before a crowd of some 50,000, nearly a fifth of the city's entire population, although now many watch it on television or listen to it on radio. Some are still too frightened of the result to either watch or listen. They simply stay at home and pray.

Nine of the ten horses and riders taking part were now corralled between two ropes at the starting and finishing point, up at the north-west corner of the Campo. The back rope had a gap in it which allowed the horses to enter. The tenth horse and its rider were still outside the back rope. This was the *rincorsa*, the horse that made the running. When it, too, came in (which it would do at high speed), the starter, a retired colonel, would depress a pedal, which made the front rope fall to the ground, and the race would begin.

The horses and their riders, known as *fantini*, were representatives of ten of the seventeen *contrade*, or districts of the city. Each *contrada* was a little world of its own, devoted since the Middle Ages to its own continuation and to the mutual good of its members, from the cradle to the grave. They are literally baptized into it on the *contrada*'s Saint's Day. It looks after them in sickness. The children play and grow up together. The women are members of the local equivalent of our Women's Institutes. Each adult contributes a regular subscription. The principal aim of a *contrada* is to win the Palio and glorify itself through victory, the culmination of days and nights of Machiavellian scheming. On the day of the Palio, husbands and wives who have married out of the *contrada* they were baptized into return to their old loyalties.

The *fantini* are mostly Sardinians. They ride *a pelo*, bareback, and without stirrups. Now, for the race, they had abandoned their pro-cessional horses and splendid uniforms for simple white doublets, with the crests of their *contrada* embroidered on them. On their heads they wore peaked metal helmets painted in their *contrada* colours. They were fitted with neck shields to protect them from the whips, which are made from the dried penises of male calves and with which the rival *fantini* belabour one another vigorously at every opportunity.

The course is three laps of the outer perimeter of the Campo, almost a kilometre, run over grey marble flags now covered with a layer of crushed, golden-yellow tufa. This is the porous earth on which, out in the country, many of the horses have carried out their training gallops. The centre of the Campo was chock full of the youth and beauty of Siena, together with several thousand assorted *wandervögeln* with huge backpacks, and souvenir and soft drink sellers. They were hemmed in by wooden stockades set up between stone pillars. On these octagonal *colonnini* boys had been squatting, frying in the sun, some of them waiting to sell these valuable hot bum/hard bum sites to the highest bidder. Those willing to spend anything between what was at that time 100,000 and 150,000 lire, depending on whether they decided to bake or sit in the shade, were accommodated on steep wooden tiers of seats which ever since the heats had begun four days before had completely obscured the lower parts of the palazzi overlooking the square. The luckiest were those who had been invited to stand high up on the velvet-draped balconies of these palazzi, who could always go inside for a *degustazione*, or what is for almost everyone else the greatest problem, a pee.

Horses and riders were now at the start more or less in the order they had been assigned by lot: the Dragon *contrada*, the Goose, the Eagle, the Panther, the Snail, the Porcupine, the Unicorn, the Giraffe, the She-Wolf and, still outside the ropes, the Forest. Only ten out of seventeen *contrade*, because to race seventeen would have been fatal. Then, without any apparent warning, Vipera, the horse of the Forest, galloped into the starting place where the other *fantini* were ramming and beating one another with their whips; the rope fell and Vipera executed a brilliant pirouette which took her across the field from left to right to race along the inner stockades, with the Goose's Tulipano di Harlem well up, together with the horses of the Dragon and the Panther.

But as the rest of the runners came into the right-angled San Martino bend at the south-east corner, which was so dangerous that its outside edge was lined with mattresses, set up to save horses and riders there from certain death, this time four horses failed to make it. One was so badly injured that it had to be put down. Of those which fell, only the Panther's Mariolina got to its feet and continued on riderless (a riderless horse can win the race). On the second circuit the She-Wolf's horse, Amore, a length behind Vipera, crashed into one of the pillars, having lost two shoes, and went down.

Vipera now had no more serious competition and his *fantino* came in to the finish with his whip held triumphantly aloft. Then the *mortaretto*, whose report put the wind up the spectators, the pigeons that get their living in the Campo and the swallows that made such a meal of the Sienese insect life, was discharged. Vipera was the winner. One minute 16.8 seconds had elapsed from start to finish.

Nineteen-year-old Bonito, born in Ronciglione near Viterbo, the youngest rider in the race, had won on the seven-year-old bay of unknown pedigree. It was the Forest's thirty-third victory since the inauguration of the Palio in 1659, their eleventh since the Second World War, their first for seven years. The Dragon's Benito, an eleven-year-old black stallion, was second, but no one cared who was second. *Vincere è tutto.* To win is everything.

But at what a cost. Five *fantini* in hospital, the Snail's Brandino put down, the Giraffe's Marilu with a ligament gone, never to run again. Bad reports, too, on Signora Lia, the Unicorn's five-year-old bay. The Italian Friends of the Earth were set to call on the authorities to suspend the next Palio.

Now the supporters of the Forest poured on to the tufa in the Campo demanding the Palio from the judges as of right with cries of '*Daccelo!*' (Give it!) and, together with Vipera and Bonito, headed off in triumph to Santa Maria di Provenzano for a Te Deum Laudamus. Afterwards they all went back to their headquarters in Via Vallepiatta for celebrations that might well have lasted for weeks.

Vipera was now a divine symbol to be paraded through the city. It had seemed to the cognoscenti that she could never run, let alone win. Two days before the race she sustained a fracture. What may have swayed the day was that during her benediction in the *contrada*'s church, San Sebastiano, she defecated generously, an exceptionally good omen, and these droppings, boxed in to discourage souvenir hunters, were still on display on the victory night.

Meanwhile, immediately after the race, fighting broke out between supporters of the Goose and the Tower. While blows were being exchanged the municipal cleaning machines entered the Campo to swallow up the rubbish. By the following morning most of the tufa would have been bulldozed from the track and by afternoon the stands would be down, with nothing to suggest that the whole colourful, violent scene would be replayed with equal passion and aggression six weeks later, on 16 August.

As the night wore on, news reached us of another inter-*contrada* battle breaking out. The police sent for extra reinforcements.

To anyone not born into a *contrada*, the Palio is a pretty rough race between pretty rough horses. What it is to the *contradaioli* is the culmination of days and nights of Byzantine scheming, in the hope of achieving glory for their district.

The head of a *contrada* is the Prior, but at the time of the Palio it is the Capitano who takes command. It is he whose task it is to *fare i partiti*, make secret agreements with other Capitani, for example to impede the victory of an hereditary enemy. This can be done by offering a good rider to a friendly *contrada* whose horse is thought to have more chance, or by denying one to a bitter rival. Huge sums of money change hands in this way.

Once a horse is consigned to its *contrada*, it is locked away in a sumptuous stable, cosseted by the equivalent of a male nurse who often sleeps in the stable with it, and guarded by a posse of extremely tough men, night and day. Each time it runs a heat, it is escorted through the narrow streets to the Campo and back by a band of *contradaioli*. We followed the fortunes of Amore, the grey stallion of the She-Wolf *contrada*, because we happened to get to know the owner.

On the night before the race each *contrada* taking part in the Palio gives a gigantic Propitiatory Dinner. We joined 980 supporters of the She-Wolf in the open air and ate a splendid meal served by women and girls of the *contrada*. There were speeches by the Prior, the Capitano and the jockey, and vast amounts of wine.

On the afternoon of the race we went to see Amore and his *fantino* blessed in the beautiful oratory of San Rocco, patron saint of the She-Wolf. Then came the solemn moment when the priest raised his right hand in benediction over Amore: 'Let this animal receive thy blessing, O Lord, whereby it may be preserved in body and freed from every harm, by the intercession of the blessed Rocco; through Christ the Lord. Amen.' Amore was sprinkled with holy water. Less than twenty-four hours later, in the heat and excitement of the race, Amore crashed into a pillar, losing two of his shoes, his balance, and the race.

Seeing the World on Two Wheels

THE FIRST two-wheeled vehicle I ever owned was the rubber-tyred scooter from Hamleys which I was given on my sixth birthday, on which I used to scoot up Castlenau. Although I loved my soundless scooter, I still envied the poor their scooters: they were built from odd bits of plank, ran on wheels retrieved from discarded roller skates and made what struck me as an attractively deafening sound as they scooted out from the slums over Hammersmith Bridge and past our flat in Castelnau in SW13 on their way to Barnes Common.

My first bike, which put me into a state of near ecstasy, was a Fairy Cycle. It had one brake which acted directly on the front tyre, which was solid. On one occasion, without telling anyone, I rode all the way from Hammersmith to Putney along the towing path, past Harrods Furniture Depository, seeing en route what looked to me like a couple of old women doing something odd with a couple of equally old-looking men behind some bushes. At that time, Barnes, especially the cemeteries on the Common, positively hummed with outdoor sexual activity.

When I was twelve, my parents bought me a bike with raised handlebars from Halfords. It cost £4 19s. 6d. At that time – the early 1930s – the cheapest bike advertised cost about £2 and came from the mysterious East. *Cycling* magazine subjected it to a test and pronounced it highly dangerous.

Two years later, I sold my Halford and, with the help of my parents and a generous uncle, bought a possibly third-hand Selbach from a boy at St Paul's. The frame was made from taper tubes so thin that they dented easily but were otherwise surprisingly strong. It had a fixed wheel, as opposed to a freewheel, alloy rims, hand-made, wired on tyres and Timken roller bearings instead of ball-bearings. It weighed about 20lb. Selbach was the Bugatti of British bike-builders. One of his machines, built in 1928, is, or was, in the Science Museum. He was killed when the front wheel of the machine he was riding got stuck in the tramlines in Kennington.

Unfortunately, I never got very far afield with my Selbach as it was almost immediately stolen. My next bike was made by the Sun Cycle and Fittings Co. and cost £7 19s. 6d. It had a Sturmey-Archer three-speed gear and moderately dropped handlebars called Lauterwassers, after a well-known English racing cyclist. On it I began to make journeys of up to 40 miles from London into the Home Counties, a lot of them on footpaths and tracks – what is known to cyclists as rough stuff. My first really long ride was to Stonehenge and back, 160 miles, half of them in the dark, in order to see the sun rise, which it failed to do while I was there as it was winter and I arrived much too early. All I can remember is the fearful cold, wondering what Druids wore under their robes to keep their spirits up, and the interminable ride home along the A303.

An even longer ride, with two other boys, was from Crickhowell on the southern side of the Black Mountains, where we had been camping, to London. One of them crashed while riding downhill at about 25mph near Monmouth, breaking nothing but his spectacles. It poured all the way across the Cotswolds and took us from 6 p.m. on a September evening until 3 p.m. the following afternoon.

When I was sixteen my father took me away from St Paul's because of my inability to pass the then equivalent of O-Level in Algebra and arranged to send me to Zurich, where I would learn the silk trade and the German language.

No doubt thinking that cycling up and down the Alps would keep my mind in wholesome channels, he allowed me to order a bicycle specially designed for this purpose from W. H. Holdsworth, a well-known bicycle-builder in Putney. It was called the Stelvio and it was fitted with a five-speed Cyclo *dérailleur* gear on which the chain derailed from one rear cog on the freewheel block to another, as such gears still do.

It would be difficult to build a more technically perfect bicycle today, except that today everything apart from the steel frame and possibly the saddle would be foreign whereas, in 1936, only British components were used. Altogether it cost £20, the equivalent of two Savile Row suits.

I did not get to the Alps for years. My father cancelled the project of my going into the silk trade in Switzerland, when he discovered that the kind of *Schweitzerdeutsch* I would learn in Zurich would make speakers of real German fall about. I sold the Stelvio in 1941, before I went abroad, thinking that I would never survive to use it again. A silly thing to do.

During the war I rode huge military bicycles with 28in wheels that weighed 60lb or more. At the Royal Military College, Sandhurst, a special drill had been evolved for manoeuvring these *poids lourds*. If you saw an officer you 'rode at attention', elongating yourself unnaturally and were lucky if you didn't fall off.

Meanwhile, a world away, in the Po Valley in Italy, Wanda was cycling with other girls through country almost identical with that equally flat country around Ferrara, depicted in Visconti's *The Garden of the Finzi-Contini*, in which similar droves of girls cycling are lovingly depicted.

Wanda's bicycle was very different to the sort of real iron I was used to pedalling. It was a single-speed Bianchi, a well-known Italian make, with an open frame, raised handlebars fitted with a wicker basket and a back-pedalling hub brake on the rear wheel, the upper parts of which were covered with thin cords to prevent the rider's skirt becoming entangled in the works.

In 1944, when her father was arrested as an anti-Fascist she and her mother were also arrested, but subsequently released. At the same time, her bicycle was confiscated. Eventually she succeeded in tracking it down to a German military headquarters where thousands of impounded bicycles were kept.

'You have stolen my bicycle,' she said to the first German officer she met there, a Colonel. Unnerved by this furious apparition, he offered her any bicycle she might fancy; she rejected the offer out of hand. Eventually, he was constrained to send for a couple of soldiers and order them to force their way through masses of bicycles to reach her own humble machine, for which she had a fierce affection. Wanda's adventures at the hands of the Germans are chronicled in her book *Peace and War: Growing up in Fascist Italy*.

After the war I was more interested in walking and running long distances than cycling. But my interest rekindled when I was sent to

New York to write about it. There I hired a bike and began sifting through the city on it, starting down by the Brooklyn Bridge and working slowly up Manhattan to that area around West 215th and 10th Avenue where the Sanitation Department performed certain rituals. And there was Harlem, beckoning or threatening?

'Don't go to Harlem,' said everyone whose judgement I valued. 'Go to Harlem,' said the detectives in the Sixteenth Precinct House, which is miles from Harlem, when I visited them, 'but keep off the sidewalks and keep your eyes off the coloured girls.' So I went and found myself the only paleface there, except those in automobiles with their windows up doing 50mph when they could to get out of the place.

In 1970 I acquired a Moulton, the only successful breakaway from the conventional conception since the invention of the Safety Bicycle, if you can forget the Velocycle, a sort of *chaise longue* fitted with wheels on which you reclined like Jean Harlow, pedalling horizontally and imbibing carbon monoxide gas at exhaust level. On the Moulton I cycled from the Wash to Wimbledon by way of the Vale of Gloucester using nothing but unclassified roads and footpaths, passing through twelve counties in four days. The present version of the Moulton looks as if it was designed by Fabergé and is, in my opinion, the most beautiful bicycle in the world.

The following year I rode to our house in Italy, near Carrara. I didn't take my Moulton because I was afraid that I wouldn't be able to find a spare tyre for the small wheel if I needed one. Instead I took a Carlton, a fine bike equipped with Campagnolo Italian components, including a 10-speed gear set-up which cost the earth, and had exactly the same trouble with the tyres that I thought I might have with the Moulton.

In France I had to replace a 27in × 1¼in tyre, a size made there only for export. This meant cycling from the Channel to the Michelin plant at Clermont Ferrand up in the Massif Central. Altogether it took me ten days to cover 1,100 kilometres and I lost three kilos in weight.

Meanwhile, Wanda had been househunting in south London, riding a borrowed pre-war Marston Golden Sunbeam, ladies' model, perhaps the best finished bicycle ever built, the sort on the male version of which curates used to drone past me on my Selbach, pushing an extremely high gear.

In 1985 Wanda and I came together for the first and what looks like being the last time as cyclists when she agreed to cycle round Ireland with me if only to 'keep me out of trobble', as she put it. For this venture we equipped ourselves with 18-speed mountain bikes built by Overbury's of Bristol. They proved unnecessarily robust even for Ireland (why people use them in cities is a mystery) and Wanda never learned to cope with the shift mechanisms which controlled the six sprockets on the freewheel block and the one on the oval Shimano triple ring chainset up front.

When beginning to go downhill she invariably pulled the left-hand lever at the same time as pushing the right-hand one forward, which transferred the chain to the lowest gear available. This left her legs whirring round without any resistance until she fell off.

At the bottom of hills she reversed the process, shifting the chain to a mighty, 48-tooth ring, at the back descending to a 14-tooth sprocket, producing the highest gear at her disposal.

At Rosscarbery she was actually blown off her bike by a freak blast of wind from the south-west which deposited her in a ditch. After five months of this, she said that in future I could get into 'trobble' by myself.

Some Canals

In the spring of 1989 I decided that I would cycle through a chunk of Europe, as far as possible making use of canal towpaths and cycle paths. Towpaths have distinct advantages for cyclists. The chances of being run over are minimal, although it is correspondingly easy to drown, and best of all they are more or less free of perceptible hills. I was very conscious of this after our experiences in Ireland, when Wanda had had such a fearful time on the Irish hills that she had vowed never to ride again, except in her native city of Parma which is dead-flat and in which you don't need a change of gear of any sort. She, she said, very firmly, would not be accompanying me.

Which was why, on a brilliant evening in late April, two of us found ourselves with our bikes, on the boat train from Liverpool to Harwich, to board the night ferry to the Hook of Holland.

The idea was to cycle from Rotterdam to Dijon, a purely arbitrary choice, which seemed to offer a variety of scenery in three countries – some of the varieties of scenery ultimately proving to be almost too great. We knew which canals had towing paths from reading a canal navigation book. What it didn't tell us was what condition they were in.

My companion was Pat Allen, an ex-Concorde pilot, who was and is very keen on food. The one thing I could be sure of was that whatever else we might lack on this journey it wouldn't be food. He loved it and communicated his enthusiasm to anyone who came within knife, fork and spoon range of him.

Pat had never done any long-distance cycling but he was, nor surprisingly, considering his profession, mad about complex mechanisms, such as multi-speed gear changers. So Charles Roberts' made-to-measure cycle workshop in the wilds of Croydon – visits to the Master are by appointment only – was a paradise for him – the equivalent to a visit to Plato's Cave, in which the prototypes displayed are, if not the ultimate in bicycles, the shadows of them. There, having been measured (I half expected Roberts to ask, as tailors do, which side we dressed), we ordered a couple of machines that were much lighter and faster than mountain bikes, were more robust than touring bikes, and were fitted with dropped handlebars. With two bikes, both painted pillarbox-red, we looked like the Trixie Sisters, stars of some circus act.

The *Konigin Beatrix*, which we boarded at Harwich, made the cross-Channel ferries I'd been on seem like convict hulks. A waiter who fulfilled my idea of an urbane Dutch bishop served us with delicious *entrecôtes* and Beaujolais Villages in a de-luxe restaurant, after which we retired to a two-berth cabin with its own shower, but not much room for our ten pieces of luggage, four pannier-bags each and two small, rather rudely named 'stuff sacks' strapped on the rear carrier. In the lavatory a sign read: *No Disposal of Unusual Things: Only Toilet Paper.*

At the Hook we pedalled out of the womb of the nice, warm *Konigin* into a freezing north wind and to a breakfast of soggy eggs on soggy bread and lukewarm coffee at the railway station. Then on to Rotterdam on a train as packed with passengers as the Piccadilly Line at 8.50, but on the surface glimpsing fishing havens, shipyards, apartment blocks, one over-sized windmill and a crazy-golf course. We were the only passengers with bikes, but not even the ticket collector, who had to force his way through the throng, said anything. Presumably because the Dutch, who own 10.5 million bikes, two for every three members of the population, regard the bicycle as sacrosanct as Hindus do cows.

In Rotterdam we stayed in a nice, small hotel in a street called the Provensinggel, on the bank of a nearby blocked-up canal, and we were told to leave our bikes in the cellar as they would certainly be pinched if we left them outside, even if locked. Large crowds assembled to admire them whenever we took them for an airing, and they, too, advised us to lock them up.

Rotterdam, almost completely destroyed by bombs in the last war, still gave the impression of being rebuilt over forty years later and the air was full of dust raised by developers excavating the foundations of enormous buildings.

We ate mussels cooked in curry sauce in a pub on the ground floor of t'Witte Hus, the first European skyscraper (1898), and saw Van Eyck's *Three Marys at the Tomb*, Brueghel's *Tower of Babel* and *The Prodigal Son* by Hieronymous Bosch, which was enough for one afternoon. We then ate a very good dinner in an animated, old restaurant – Zealand fish soup, *filet d'agneau*, *crêpes au citron* – everyone talking nineteen to the dozen with their mouths full, which can be a bit messy in Dutch. By 11 p.m. the streets were utterly deserted. What the local inhabitants were up to was anybody's guess.

From Rotterdam we cycled through the Delta, across dams and barrages, one of them being known as the Stopcock of the Netherlands, built after 1953 when floods drowned thousands of people and left huge tracts of Holland's most fertile land under water.

In the course of these three days a freezing north wind blew, in which daffs – it was supposed to be spring – and all other living things, except coot, shelduck, herons and gulls, kept a low profile, and it drove us before it without the necessity of pedalling. From time to time we were overtaken by elderly Dutch ladies, some of them in national garb, and mounted on bikes that looked like two harps welded together.

You could see for ever but for much of the time there wasn't much to see. The little ports that had inspired eighteenth-century marine painters were no more. The general effect was ever so slightly depressing.

At Renesse, a sort of mini-Margate, we bought beer, bratwurst and portions of eel and crab from a fast-food place and, next door, lanolin and half a litre of benzine for Pat's bum, which was having saddle trouble. At Middelburg, a town with concentric rings of medieval houses, mostly destroyed by the Germans and rebuilt, we stayed in a pretty little hotel, named after the church, the Biji de Abdij, for 30 guilders (about £11.50) each.

From Vlissingen on Walcheren Island – a big, green belfry, big, old tiled houses – we crossed the Westerschelde to Breskens and followed a cyclepath through monotonous green, vegetable country to Sluis on the Dutch–Belgian frontier. Here, a striped, sliding bar separated the two countries so we slid it open and entered Belgium – and slid it shut again. There was no one to ask for our passports which, back in 1989, was noteworthy, and no one did during the entire trip.

We zoomed into the heart of Bruges on an asphalt towing path along a magnificent stretch of canal lined with tall black poplars and gloomy fishermen. We spent two nights in Bruges. The Hospital of St John at Bruges houses the majority of Memling's masterpieces, and a lot of time is needed to ponder on his mysterious origins and extraordinary achievements. Among other wonders was a pub serving 300 different kinds of Belgian beer, horse-carriages driven by bottle-nosed coachmen, and a restaurant – De Coninc, Breidelstraat – which provided us with a bucket of mussels each (the restaurant's annual consumption is 20,000 kilos a year) cooked in an onion and celery soup sauce.

Meanwhile, with the aid of a carillon of 47 bells, 366 steps overhead, a *carilloneur* was murdering Bach and Beethoven.

Then from Bruges to Ghent we took a towpath much of the way rendered almost impassable by furrows and pot-holes. In the canal there were 2,000-ton barges, with washing hung up to dry (by Mr Toad?). We arrived in Ghent by way of a decayed industrial area lined with mean terrace houses.

The next day – Ghent is nice but Bruges is nicer – in the teeth of a strong, south-west wind, we rode an almost unridable towpath through a nightmare industrial landscape, under motorways where there were piles of horrible old mattresses, to pick up a marvellous asphalt towpath on the bank of the canalized River Escaut. On it there were hundreds of cyclists all dressed – young and old – for racing, and all mounted on what must have amounted to about £150,000 worth of racing bikes.

The next day, after a long stretch of good towpath on the Escaut, we crossed the Belgian–French frontier near Bleharies where there were lots of big barges moored, with cars and bad-tempered dogs on deck, and the pub was bursting its seams with barge people who were more friendly than their pets. It was Sunday morning.

Here, by mistake, we got on to the Scarpe Canal, which passes through a really spooky, completely finished industrial area, which would have landed us at Arras, far to the west. Eventually we managed to get back to the Escaut, west of Vincennes, after a difficult cross-country route which passed through a region of huge heaps of reject coal, great ponds full of bright green effluent, chemical plants and refineries, some of them closed for ever, dangerous-looking youths, and signs which read *Danger de Mort*.

'You're some picker, Newby, when it comes to routes,' Pat said, and it was difficult to disagree with him. At this moment we heard a cuckoo and saw a bluebell which had lost its colour.

At Cambrai the hotel, Le Cluny, had no food and our room was on the third floor, reached by a spiral staircase, and was the only place to leave our bicycles. By the time we had carried them up, together with eight pannier-bags and two stuff sacks, we were done in. To revive ourselves we had a huge dinner and two bottles of Chinon at 395 French francs (£39.50) for two.

At Cambrai we picked up the St Quentin Canal, which winds its way through nice country around what was the easternmost part of the salient created when British tanks were first used in 1917, open, sometimes pretty country which has a number of British cemeteries hidden away in it.

Thirty kilometres south of Cambrai the canal enters Le Grand Souterrain, a tunnel 5,670 metres long and then a second one, Le Tronquoy, both of which formed part of the Hindenburg Line, Germany's almost impregnable defensive system on the Western Front, only finally broken by the Allies in 1918. I shall always remember the walk through Le Tronquoy, which is 1,098 metres long and pitch-black – pushing our loaded bikes along a four-feet-wide path littered with lumps of wood and metal, five feet above the water, was really hair-raising.

South of St Quentin, the only canal of any use to us on our way to the Canal de Bourgogne and Dijon, was the Canal latéral à l'Oise, which, according to our canal guides, would, after thirty-four not very attractive kilometres, dump us in the canalized, not all that beautiful either, Oise, which, in turn, 104 kilometres later, would precipitate us into the Seine downstream from Paris, which was not where we wanted to be.

We resolved this problem by recklessly hiring a van and driving it to Villers-Cotterets near the headwaters of the Canal de L'Ourcq. This Arcadian little canal, which for much of its course runs through tunnels of trees, as most French canals tend to do, at one point almost collides with the Marne (at Nanteuil-le-Haudouin), and it was to this place that General Gallieni, military governor of Paris, sent 600 Parisian taxis loaded with 6,000 *poilus* to reinforce the line, saving the day in 1914.

Eventually its towpath took us under the *autoroutes* west of Paris at Pont de Bondy, which is decorated with inspired graffiti, and delivered us into the Bassin de la Villette, in an area of Paris in which, once, all you could hope for was not to be taken apart, but which by 1989, with the building of the Cité des Sciences, was rapidly becoming positively respectable. From the Bassin the Canal St Martin conducted us to the Seine beyond the Place de la Bastille.

As the Seine has no towpath, we took a train from the Gare de Lyon to Sens on the beautiful, canalized River Yonne and followed it to its junction with the Canal de Bourgogne at Migennes, along some of the most difficult, overgrown towpaths of the entire route, but worth it.

It took us three days to follow the Canal de Bourgogne up past 113 locks to the 378-metre, summit-level tunnel at Pouilly-en-Auxois – a place with a name that makes you think that it must have the most wonderful little restaurant – well, it hasn't. On the way we became embrambled where the towpath petered out because we were on the wrong side of the canal, which involved us in horrible, unridable excursions through fields.

From Pouilly we swooped down the beautiful valley of the Ouche past 167 locks, through endless enfilades of trees, the latter part grotesquely overhung by the *autoroute*, to Dijon where we took a train to Paris. The next day we had a frightening bike ride along the quais and across the Seine to Porte Maillot, the airport bus terminal, where the bus people aren't all that mad about bikes. At Charles de Gaulle, British Airways wanted us to take the pedals off but we told them we didn't have the right tools.

Altogether we covered about 650 miles in a fortnight, not including van and train rides, with no punctures. The peace and quiet of travelling along towpaths, even if they sometimes become impassable, has to be experienced to be believed. Neither of us would want to ride the Belgian and northern French sections again though, some of which are only suitable for making horror films. If we did it again, we would start somewhere south of Paris and perhaps end up in Switzerland.

Our choice of stopping places was governed by their proximity to the canal. The same applied to ancient monuments and restaurants. We ate well, but, surprisingly, scarcely anything memorable, apart from the mussels, which was rather disappointing. You can't carry guide books gastronomical or otherwise to three countries on a bike because of the weight – a canal guide book is the most important item.

Pat was a really dab hand at navigation because he had been a flight navigator before becoming a pilot. He had a circular computer which he used to point down some idyllic, tree-lined canal reach, and then announce that in an hour and twenty minutes we would arrive at such and such a place, a piece of Concordean magic that never ceased to amaze me. It was a pity that he couldn't locate restaurants with it.

The Land of the Camels

WE WERE out in the sticks, which were very abundant up in Northern Rajasthan, about 150 miles from the Pakistan border. Our vehicle was a Hindustan Ambassador, a faithful copy of an early 1950s Morris Oxford. The driver was also a faithful copy of every other early 1950s vintage driver we had ever travelled with in India.

We were heading south-westwards, towards Ajmer. To the left, running in the same direction, was the Aravalli Range, the only mountain range in Rajasthan, which is what used to be known as Rajputana, and the oldest mountain range in the world.

It is, therefore, not surprising that having been where it is for some 700 million years – it originally extended from the Kumaon Himalaya to the southern end of the Indian peninsula – it is now the colour of old bones and so worn down that it rarely exceeds 3,000 feet (Mount Abu is 5,000 feet but is detached from the main range).

The Aravalli begin near Delhi and finally expire on the inner edge of the Rann of Kutch, a spooky, 8,000-square-mile expanse of saline marsh or saline desert, according to the time of year, which borders on the Arabian Sea, south of Karachi, in Gujarat (and is, or was – nothing is for ever – populated with wild asses, which must be one of the few places remaining in India where they have a chance of not being mucked about).

The only river of any value in this part of Rajasthan is the Luni. It rises near Pushkar, which we were on our way to visit, and it, too, ends up in the Rann of Kutch. On its banks, before it becomes brackish further downstream, barley and wheat can be grown, the only place in Northern Rajasthan where this is possible. Apart from this fertile bit the whole of Northern and Western Rajasthan is a vast, more or less sandy tract.

It was midday in mid-November 1989 and the temperature was still about 32°C (89.6°F), and whatever anyone tells you at this time of year there is no need to wrap up well in the evenings. This is a region of extremes. In May/June, when no sane traveller would be here, the main day temperature is 94°F, but it can and does go up to 120°F, which is insupportable unless you are a fire worshipper. In December/January you really need your woollies, when the night temperature often falls below freezing. October–March are the best months in Rajasthan.

We were in the midst of seemingly endless expanses of sandy semi-desert, but one in which, in spite of being a semi-desert, equally endless groves of trees gave merciful shade and a touch of variety to what would otherwise have been an utterly monotonous landscape, and, goodness knows, it was monotonous enough even with them.

They were pretty trees, at a distance a bit reminiscent of olives. From time to time they were rigorously pruned so that their leaves could be used as feed for the animals and after this was done they looked terrible, like trees after an artillery bombardment.

Under them were flocks of sheep, bred mostly for their wool, goats that had done their best to make the semi-desert what it is and had every intention of keeping it that way, great herds of camels, of what looked like various degrees of domesticity, the same colour as the sand, which did all the pulling and ploughing here and, rather surprisingly, cows.

At that season, apart from some stunted shrubs, some clumps of coarse grass, and what looked like pampas grass, the only real colour in that wilderness was provided by the people who lived in it – the women loaded with chunky jewellery which must have weighed a ton and would have done well in Van Cleef and Arpels, all dressed in the brilliantly coloured wraps which took the place of saris; the men in their equally dazzling headcloths, in shades of pink and green and every other conceivable colour under the sun, which there, in the land of the Rajputs, seemed to be twice the size of similar headgear worn anywhere else in India.

There were few enough hamlets, let alone villages, and those that could be seen from the road mostly consisted of mud huts roofed with thatch and were so far apart that you wondered how anyone ever got to the intervening fields to work them.

In fact the only reason why those habitations were where they were was because there was water. If it failed, as it sometimes did, then the occupants moved.

In that part of Rajasthan almost all the surface water was brackish and on the borders of Jaipur and Jodhpur we passed Lake Sambhar which produced large quantities of salt, said to be carried to it on the wind from the Rann of Kutch. Some rainwater was collected in reservoirs called *johras*.

The wells were unique. They were so beautiful to look at that when you first set eyes on them, you thought that you were looking at some sort of domed tomb or temple. The shaft itself was surrounded by four slender columns that resembled minarets, or sometimes there were only two, one on either side of it. The water from these wells was, and in some cases still is, raised to the surface in leather waterskins by bullocks driven down an inclined ramp. The wells were popular meeting places and at each one there was a shrine to Hanuman, the Monkey God, who was much venerated by the Rajputs who lived there.

The only crop in the semi-desert was millet, although gram-chick pea was grown for fodder. The monsoon rains began, that is if they came at all, towards the second half of September, and continued, more off than on, until the beginning of November, but never amounted to more than ten inches a year, more often five. The rain gods were invoked with the air of fire. The sands were ploughed with wooden ploughs pulled by camels. Only a few showers were needed to bring the crop to maturity.

To the north and west of where we were, somewhere north of Ajmer, was the Thar, the Indian Desert, the Sanskrit name for which, pre-dating any other, is Marusthali, which signifies Death. The Thar separates India from Pakistan along a 300-mile front and its sands, wind-borne, make deep inroads into the semi-desert and in some places, where we were then, the roads were partially blocked by it.

It was an awe-inspiring sight: long, straight, parallel ridges of sand, each one up to a couple of miles long, as regularly spaced as ripples on a seashore, their summits, blown up to a height of between fifty and a hundred feet by the prevailing westerly winds, were constantly on the move. Difficult to believe that a friendly monsoon could turn it into a temporary paradise of succulent vegetation for sheep and cattle almost overnight.

There were a lot of birds in the semi-desert: peacocks in thousands, regarded as inviolable by Hindus, made the air hideous with their screaming, and there were partridges and Indian rollers. We also saw nilgai, a sort of deer.

Most of the inhabitants were Hindus, although it was the Rajputs of the warrior (Kshatriya) caste who still had the most clout, as they had done since time immemorial. To them, rather like Scottish chieftains, riches have always been less important than birth and martial prowess. Their clansmen could be penniless but they were just as welcome at the chief's house.

Like the Normans, these Rajputs were mighty fortress builders. The fortresses looked impregnable with their gates covered with iron plates and spikes at an appropriate level to discourage elephants from bashing them in with their heads. Some of them had huge catchment systems which delivered the rainwater to cisterns underneath the courtyards.

Some of these fortresses looked impregnable but they were not always so. If they were penetrated by the enemy, usually Muslims, the Rajput garrisons, their robes stained with bright yellow turmeric, the garb of doom, and inflamed by large doses of *bhang* (hashish), fought to the last, leaving their women to practise *jauhar*, self-immolation on a great pyre, taking their children with them.

But not every Rajput fought to the last man, or the last woman. Sometimes, when forced out of their positions by Muslim *force majeure*, they either managed to found a new town or city, or else went off to serve as soldiers of fortune either with those who had defeated them, or any other employers who could afford their services.

That afternoon we arrived in Ajmer, late as we invariably were whenever we travelled by car in Rajasthan, due to events beyond anyone's control. This time the sump fell off and a back wheel ran over it, squashing it flat, a mishap unusual even for India.

It took two sump beaters three and a half hours to unsquash it and then it wouldn't fit. Eventually a replacement was found in a dump full of old, wrecked Ambassadors, where any sane person would have looked in the first place.

No time, in Ajmer, to visit the Dargah, burial place of Khwaja Muin ud din Chishti, a Sufi saint (1143–1235), whose shrine is regularly visited by innumerable Muslims, many of whom travel long distances on foot.

Akbar, who used to come every year from Agra, built a mosque there; Shah Jahan built another; Humayun completed the shrine and the Nizam of Hyderabad had the doors made which are now covered with horse shoes nailed to them by horse copers in memory of successful deals.

No time either to visit the mosque called Adhai-din-ka-Jhopra, otherwise the 'hut of two and a half days', which was what it took to build it. A bit slow considering that it was all done supernaturally.

Why no time? Because in order to get to Pushkar we had another seven miles to go; the sun was already sinking in the west, and when we got there we had to find a tent reserved for us in a tented village set up by Rajasthan Tourism, one of 600 more or less identical tents, not *une mince affaire* (an insignificant manner) after nightfall, as one French couple described it to us the following morning, having been faced with the necessity of doing just this.

And so we set off along the beautiful shores of the Ana Sagar, a lake made in the twelfth century by damming the river Luni, the one that flows into the Rann of Kutch, which had a luxury hotel on its shores and two marble pavilions built by Shah Jahan in 1637.

Then the Ambassador ground up over a rocky saddle in the Nag Pahar, the Snake Mountain, and after a long freewheel downhill we found ourselves in the environs of Pushkar where the Fair was going full blast. It had already been going on for seven days.

This was the night of 12–13 November and four o'clock on the morning of the 13th would be Kartik Purnima, the auspicious moment of the full moon of Kartik (October/November) when every Hindu present in and around Pushkar at that moment would be trying to bathe in the Pushkar Sarowar, the sacred lake.

Pushkar lies between ranges of stony mountains with the lake hidden away below it to the south, and it is overlooked by two steep hills with temples on top of them – the one to the south-west is the Ratnagiri Hill which supports the temple of Savitri. To the west of the village the great sand dunes of the Thar desert begin.

At this moment, around five o'clock in the evening, there was not much to see of Pushkar, what with about 200,000 Rajasthani and other assorted pilgrims on its doorsteps, hordes of sadhus down from the Himalayas (one of them hanging in a tree), innumerable merchants in innumerable booths selling all sorts of merchandise, including trappings for camels and cattle, not all of it tourist junk, plus thousands of foreign tourists. (The Rajasthan Tourist Authority estimated 100,000 for the whole fair, but one never quite believes hundreds of thousands and millions in India.)

The tented camp was on the edge of the sands with the temple of Savitri looming up behind it on its hill. On them a large proportion of the 200,000 humans, together with something like 50,000 camels, cows, bullocks, calves, sheep, goats and horses were encamped, together with the carts in which they had come, some hauled by bullocks, some by camels, a few by tractors.

The sun was setting now, a big, red blood orange that looked as if it was floating in a jar of honey, and the smoke of whatever number of camp fires 200,000 people need to cook their evening meals, rose in the air, together with all the noises that domestic animals make before settling down for the night, grunts and groans and the excruciating noise made by one camel which, for some reason, was having its nostrils pierced. Soon it was quite dark.

The de luxe tents were not all that luxe, but how can you make a tent luxe in the middle of a sandy waste unless it has a wooden floor? They were laid out on a simple grid-iron plan but nevertheless it was difficult to find one's own and we had some interesting encounters with various Japanese, Swedes, Americans, Germans and Brits in the course of looking for it, some of them being without clothes.

Take a big plastic bag, if you are a luxe tent inhabiter, or a non-luxe one for that matter, as it is almost impossible to find a dustbin. The loos were some way off but, once there, you could get hot water for washing, brewed up on an open fire.

The principal problem was to know what to do with one's valuables as tents don't have locks. There were some strong boxes in 'Reception' but they were usually full, so you had to carry anything you didn't want to lose with you. In fact we didn't hear of anyone being robbed. There were also dormitory sleeping tents which were much cheaper.

Serve-yourself meals were taken in a huge, communal, gaily-coloured tent, most dishes of Indian inspiration – vegetables only and no alcoholic drinks in it or anywhere else in Pushkar. The food was not bad. The bathing began at 4 a.m., with the huge full moon of Kartik overhead, from the twenty-five bathing ghats which almost entirely surround it.

This is the most sacred lake in the whole of India, the place where
Lord Brahma, Creator of the Universe, while flying overhead on his
tame goose, dropped a lotus petal while searching for a suitable place
to perform a yagna (a Vedic sacrifice). Where the petal landed the lake
appeared and there Brahma landed to perform it.

In order to perform the yagna satisfactorily it was necessary for Savitri,
Brahma's wife, to be present, but she took so long to get ready that
Brahma used a complaisant milkmaid as a stand-in. By the time Savitri
arrived the whole thing was over.

She put a curse on Brahma to the effect that henceforth he would
only be worshipped in Pushkar, and today the Brahma temple there is
the only temple in India in which he is worshipped. Savitri then left for
the Ratnagiri Hill, above the lake, one of the two now crowned with
temples, and there immolated herself in one of those feats of combustion
so irresistible to Hindu gods and goddesses.

Watching this vast concourse of brilliantly clad bathers entering the
turgid waters of the lake, hour after hour, for it is impossible for 200,000
people to do so at one time, I couldn't help worrying about a passage
in Murray's great *Handbook for Travellers in India, Pakistan, Burma and
Ceylon*, 19th edition, 1962. It reads: 'The sacred crocodiles in the lake
will be fed by the Mahants [the guardians of the temples] on request,
when a small gratuity of one or two rupees will be appropriate.' I hoped
that this information was out of date.

For much of the rest of the day we sat out under a canvas tilt on top
of a sandhill, in what was a temporary teahouse, drinking endless cups
of what I thought was a delicious beverage which didn't taste of anything
recognizable, certainly not tea.

From this eminence, looking out towards the temple of Savitri on
the hill above, we watched the owners putting their camels through
their paces for prospective customers, or consulting a team of Brahman
astrologers out on the sands about prospects for the Hindu equivalent
of 1990.

The closing ceremony took hours and ran late. We left after a great
tug-of-war between a hastily assembled team of young memsahibs from
all over the world and their tough Rajasthani equivalents, which ended
in a draw.

We stayed on the hill until the moment when the sun sank and the moon, now on the wane, was already high in the sky behind it. Then we churned our way through the sand, back through the encampments from which the country people were now in full retreat in bullock and camel carts and painted buses that looked like brilliant insects. It was all over. In all our lives we had seldom enjoyed ourselves more.

The Land
of the Elephants

THE ELEPHANTS, a couple of dozen of them, lay in the river, partly submerged, being scrubbed by their attendants, looking rather like a lot of old wooden ships being careened. Others constantly arrived and departed.

From time to time they emitted submarine gurgling noises. They sounded contented, but you can never be sure about elephants. At other times they uttered shrill, ear-splitting trumpeting sounds but whether these indicated rage or joy was impossible to say, unless you had an intimate knowledge of elephants, which most people, even those brought up on the Babar books, do not.

If they were displeased, it was probably only because their attendants – two scrubbers and the driver, the mahout; there were three men for each one of them – were trying to move them from some nook in the river bed which they found comfortable to another less so in order to get their brushes to one of those parts which even an elephant with a proboscis around six feet long cannot reach easily.

It takes anything from an hour to an hour and a half to scrub an elephant thoroughly from stem to stern and that year 134 had to be given the treatment twice a day, at sunrise and sunset, for anything up to a month.

Sometimes, while being bathed they rolled over on their stomachs, and drew their front legs up under them – the first stage for an elephant in the process of rising up on all four feet. Often this was just a fun-loving feint to keep their keepers guessing, and they subsided again. Even when lying, apparently semi-comatose, in the water their trunks were seldom still. Most of the time they used them to form graceful arabesques and curlicues, sometimes ganging up with others to produce continuous animate friezes. Or else they used them to squirt jets of water high in the air, looking like exotic fountains of a sort that the Sun King might have commissioned for Versailles if he had been interested in elephants.

Most of these elephants had the upper parts of their trunks and their ears covered with multicoloured decorations, moons and stars and so on, in what must have been waterproof pigments as they appeared to survive multiple immersions. Some of these embellishments were so finely executed that they looked more like the work of a tattooist than someone working with a brush.

The elephants were at Sonepur for the Mela, the great cattle fair which some say is still the biggest in all Asia. It lasts up to a month and reaches its height on Kartik Purnima, the first full moon after Diwali (the fetsival of lights), which corresponds in our calendars to October/ November. That year, it fell on 13 November.

Sonepur is a small place on the right bank of the River Gandak in Bihar, the most depressed and worst administered state in the whole of India – and the most corrupt, which is saying something. In the November elections which were held about the same time as my visit, a number of condemned criminals – not political prisoners – stood on the Congress ticket while still in jail.

The Gandak rises in Nepal, 430 miles to the north, and at Sonepur it joins the Ganges, opposite Patna. At this point the Ganges, already augmented by two other large rivers, the Gogra and the Son, rises thirty feet when the rains come in June. It runs at a rate of more than a million cubic feet a second – more than the maximum discharge of the Mississippi. But in mid-November it is more or less low water.

At around eight o'clock in the morning, when the fog which had blotted out everything was at last pierced by the sun rising across the river, everything turned to pure gold: the expanses of mud which formed its banks, the normally dun-coloured river, thick with silt, churning its way downhill with the Ganges towards the Bay of Bengal; the devotees dunking themselves in it and making oblations; the elephants that now looked like big, smooth rocks embedded in it; even the jet-black water buffaloes that had been brought down by their herdsmen for a more perfunctory wash were golden. The two girder bridges which spanned the river sixty feet or so overhead had become golden, too. The bridges, with supporting piers sunk a hundred feet or more in the river bed, were miracles of pre-First World War engineering. This was still a very heavily used railway – until 1950 when the Swedes built a railway platform 2,470 feet long at Storvik, the platform at Sonepur was the longest in the world at 2,415 feet.

Long freight trains, and more infrequently passenger trains, some of them hauled by big WP- and WG-class steam locomotives, rumbled out through the webs of golden girders between the spans, their drivers making them whistle mournfully as only Indian drivers really know how to do.

The Mela takes place in a series of mango groves which altogether cover more than a hundred acres, and even when the temperature is up to 25°C (around 77°F), which it often is here in November, the leaves of these trees, some of which are more than 300 years old, give such a deep, dark shade that it is like being underwater.

This is where the animals were tethered, or hobbled, in their thousands. The cows and their calves, some with a hump, some without, those without them perhaps a mixture of English and Indian strains that were originally bred in the mid-nineteenth century by William Taylor, the then Commissioner for Patna. Whatever their origins, most wore garlands of marigolds and had their horns painted in exotic shades of mauve and shocking pink.

The cows most holy were sold for their milk, bullocks for ploughing and hauling the carts which are the staple transport of rural India, buffaloes for heavy ploughing. There were enclaves of donkeys and ponies and the camp of the elephants, down by the river.

It was difficult to know how many animals there were at any one time because they were constantly on the move in and out of the fairground. The only figures I have are for forty years ago, 1958/9, when 2,500 ponies and horses, 1,675 buffaloes, an astonishing 81,675 cows and bullocks and 500 elephants changed hands. At Sonepur in 1989, buffaloes were fetching between 7,000 rupees (about £27) and 12,000 rupees (£46); cows and bullocks between 10,000 and 12,000 rupees; ponies up to 30,000 rupees – there were better ponies and horses for sale at Jaipur in Rajasthan, where polo was played, and at Calcutta where they raced them. The price for elephants was around a lakh of rupees (getting on for £400, a lakh being 100,000 rupees. A lot of money in India.

The noise at the Mela ground was indescribable, what with the braying of donkeys in need of sympathy, the whinnying of high-stepping ponies as they were unwillingly ridden up and down under the mango trees, being shown off to prospective customers, the rumbling of the trains on the embankments overhead, the ear-shattering music from the loud-speakers that were everywhere – all Indians are deaf from birth to any sound of 100 decibels and over, which is the equivalent to being ten feet from a pneumatic drill. The year before my visit there was an additional torment, political candidates in jeeps drawing attention to their merits with the aid of loud hailers. This is not to speak of some 30,000 people all clearing their throats, the screeching sounds made by a big dipper in one of the fairgrounds as it went into a what sounded like terminal dive, and Sivite and Vishnuvite holy men blowing on conches and banging gongs.

You had to be careful also where you put your feet. A thousand dung fires were burning at any one time and they tended to hide from view the women with small babies who crouched in the dust selling sugar, bananas, sugar cane and such, and who could easily be crushed under-foot by a European such as myself, wearing size 12s. Even more danger-ous was that large tracts of the Sonepur Mela grounds, which included the entire river front for a mile or more up and downstream, were no-go areas – the places to which Indians went in countless thousands when about their business. From what one could see most of them suffered from the kind of trouble that wiped out, and still does, large numbers of Indians and Europeans. It was a sort of *Côte d'Ordures*.

Sonepur is a place of great sanctity to Hindus, partly because this is the confluence of the Gandak with the Ganges, which is always the mark of a holy place; but also because in Hindu myth, it was the site of a great battle between the Lord of the Elephants and the Lord of the Crocodiles, which was won by the Elephants with the support of Vishnu and Siva.

At the confluence of the two rivers a temple, the Harihar Nath temple, which houses the images of Vishnu and Siva, commemorates this tem-porary thaw in what was otherwise a more or less permanent cold war between them and their supporters.

In 1989 the great bathing day had been Kartik Purnima, 13 November, and on it 200,000 people were reputed to have taken to the water, commemorating the Triumph of Good over Evil. According to most

Hindu observers, who are conditioned by their own holy writ which rarely deals in five figures when six will do, all bathing ceremonies involve either 200,000 persons, or otherwise a million, or multiples of a million. The cattle fair itself is supposed to attract a million visitors and probably does over the period it lasts.

It was now 16 November, three days after the great bathing day at Sonepur, on which date we had been at the camel fair at Pushkar in Rajasthan more than 600 miles to the north-west, which also comes to a climax on the same day; and what had been the estimated 200,000 bathers were now reduced to a few dozen.

But however much we enjoyed looking at the cows and the bullocks and the buffaloes and the horses and the donkeys, what we really liked best was watching the elephants, dangerous as they were.

Every year at Sonepur a spectator or two and a mahout or two are killed by elephants, and some of them have been responsible for multiple killings, And it was to them, in their camp near the temple of Harihar Nath, where they were chained up under the trees, that we always returned, often to find some of them fast asleep, looking innocent and leaning on some unfortunate mango trees which could only just support their weight.

The most wonderful things about them are their trunks which, according to the French anatomist, Baron Cuvier, are made up of about 40,000 closely interlaced muscles, the tip of which is the elephantine equivalent to the human hand, with a finger-like extremity and the equivalent of a thumb and two openings of the nostrils through which it can breathe when swimming with only the tip of the trunk above water, as a sort of snorkel.

If it so wishes it can, like a camel, fill a cavity which is separated from its stomach and which holds ten gallons of water and then bring it back up through its trunk and give itself a shower on land. With its trunk injured an elephant is helpless, which is why it always keeps it high in the air when confronted by a tiger, using its tusks to deal with it.

An elephant with tusks that are turned upwards and outwards is capable of hurling a tiger thirty feet. If they are turned down, it endeavours to pin the tiger to the ground with them and crush it. An Indian elephant can lift a log weighing half a ton using a tusk; but if its tusk is damaged it becomes uncontrollable with rage, as it does when in must, a state of frenzy which only affects males.

Normally it forages for its own food but those in captivity, such as those at Sonepur, have their meals prepared for them, which amounts to about 224lbs of special grass a day, and about half a bushel of grain. They are also partial to sugar cane and they loved the bananas we gave them, both of which grow hereabouts in abundance.

Most of these elephants were about 10½ft high when fully grown. Only the males had tusks, but there are some naturally tuskless males, known as *muknas*.

Elephants are polygamous. Females can breed from the age of fifteen onwards and the gestation period is twenty-one months. Their young suckle with their mouths not their trunks. Their cheek teeth follow the arc of a circle and are a continuous growth so that only one or part of two are emergent and in use at any one time. They are prone to various diseases but can live up to seventy years, but only if given soft food in old age. So much for Indian elephants.

Facing them, sitting in the mouths of their tents, and watching them all day, that is when they are not down at the river, were the owners, most of them flinty-eyed, feudal Rajput *zamindars*, landlords, who employ what are known as Babu Sahibs – literally Mr Clerks – to do their dirty work.

Very elegant some of the owners were, dressed in cream silk, Nehru-type jackets. Some of them had automatic pistols stuck in their belts, and so did their retainers. They were a nasty-looking lot.

These men acquire elephants for prestige reasons, just as some Midland manufacturer might buy a Bugatti or an Isotta Fraschini, not to drive it but to contemplate it, and this is just what they did every day from first to last light. Most of them had no intention of selling their elephants, unless it was to acquire a more prestigious model.

One elephant, although we never actually met it, had been marched 1,000 miles to be present at the Mela. We did, however, meet a ten-year-old bull who had walked 400 miles in fifteen days and would soon be setting off on his way home, unless someone made an offer for him that his owner couldn't refuse.

Several of the Babu Sahibs said that they were having difficulty in replenishing their stocks, now that the taking of wild ones was no longer possible. One said that the Mela was rapidly declining in size and importance, and the number of elephants on show was much diminished. In 1988 there had been more than 200. This year, 1989, there were only 134.

Since 1976, when the Government amended the property laws, the Babu Sahibs have had to adopt extraordinary measures in order to evade taxation. They now operate a system known as *Beenami* (literally, 'In Someone Else's Name'), in which they hand over their land not only to non-existent persons but also to their dogs and cats and other animals, possibly elephants. So much for Babu Sahibs. Give me an elephant any day.

Two Degrees West

meridian n. One of the imaginary lines joining the north and south poles at right angles to the equator.

Collins English Dictionary

The Equatorial Circumference of the Earth is 24,901.8 English Miles, divided into 360 Degrees of Longitude, each of 69.17 English (or 60 Geographical Miles; these Degrees are measured from the Meridian of Greenwich, and numbered East and West of that point to meet in the Antipodes (a point or place diametrically opposite to another on the surface of the earth) at the 180th Degree . . .

Whitaker's Almanac

By the decision of a conference of delegates from almost all the civilised countries in the world held at Washington in 1884, the meridian of Greenwich was accepted as the universal prime meridian from which longitudes were measured to +180 (E.180) and −180 (W.180). The French delegate dissented and in France maps continued to be drawn to the prime meridian in Paris . . . In 1911 France adopted the Greenwich meridian.

Chamber's Encyclopaedia, vol. 8, 1950

FOR THE NEWBYS, the latter part of 1990 and a large part of 1991 added up to what my Scandinavian and Finnish shipmates used to describe (in their case it was 1939, which they were already bellyaching about on January 1st) as a 'focking, no-good year'.

At the end of 1990 Wanda was badly bitten by a monkey on a railway station while we were on our way to the source of the Ganges, where we had hoped to encounter some Hindu holy men. Instead, she had to embark on a course of rabies injections. By the time these were finished the part of the Himalayas above Gangotri we had been bound for was buried in snow and the temple had closed for the winter.

I was next, struck down by some never-to-be identified Indian malady a couple of days before we returned to England, which left me for months unable to write. It was a no-good year but when you think of what can befall you in India, it might have been much worse.

By the autumn of 1991 I had begun to feel better, and once more had the feeling that I would like to travel, not in India or some other, far-off foreign place, but through England, the greener, wilder parts of it if possible, and the sooner the better as I was knocking seventy-two.

What I now had to decide was how much of England I was going to take in while travelling through it; whether I was going to walk it or bike it; and who could I find barmy enough to go with me – I didn't fancy long, solitary evenings thumbing through old magazines or watching TV.

As usual, whenever I begin to think about going on a journey, there was not much time left for me to make up my mind as to where I was going and how I was going to do it. It was now late October. I either had to begin the journey in November, or wait until the following spring, which in England was not likely to start until after Easter.

Why November anyone might quite reasonably ask? Because I wanted to do it now and not wait for the spring. And because it is only between November and March that you stand any chance at all of finding a bed and breakfast, without booking it in advance, which can be a difficult thing to do. And in spring and summer I had to garden.

There are other advantages. Autumn and winter are the only times of year when the locals have any time for travellers. For the rest of the year you are regarded as one of a vast army of grockles, otherwise tourists. But November might already be too late if the snow fell early in the Pennine Chain. I was already set on traversing more or less the length of England from north to south. That way you have the comforting impression of going downhill.

I consulted the *Readers' Digest Complete Atlas of the British Isles*. Published in the 1960s, it is packed with information, some of it highly eccentric, concerning, among other subjects, what we eat, where you might find a giant goby fish, electric rays, and the 14 different sorts of bats and butterflies. From it you could also learn about the commonest reasons for having to see a doctor, dialects, folklore, the meanings of place names and people's names, the number of different religions, the sorts of crime you might have to put up with in any particular area, and the birthplaces of illustrious persons.

Much of this information was by now, in 1991, unfortunately out of date, the statistics having been compiled in 1964. But the maps were still good and a fold-out section showed Britain in relief.

The *Atlas* showed that the northernmost point of England on the border with Scotland is on the coast about 2¾ miles north-east of Berwick-on-Tweed. It also showed that Berwick-on-Tweed, which many people think is in Scotland, is neatly bisected by the meridian two degrees west of Greenwich.

This particular meridian, not having crossed dry land previously on its way south from the North Pole through the Arctic Ocean, emerges on it for the first time in Aberdeenshire at Kinnairds Head near Fraser-burgh, on the North Sea. After about twenty miles or so on land it sinks into the sea on the sands at Foveran Links, at the mouth of a beautiful estuary north of Aberdeen; and it makes its début on English soil about three-quarters of a mile north of Berwick-on-Tweed at a place marked on the 1¼″ to the mile Ordnance Survey map for this part of the world as Brotherston's Hole.

Where would I end up, I wondered, if I followed Two Degrees West southwards through England to the point where, presumably, it took off across the English Channel for some part of France?

When I looked it up on the southern England sheet of the *Atlas*, I couldn't believe it. It actually exited for France a couple of miles or so from where we lived in Dorset, a few hundred yards east of a cliff known as Dancing Ledge.

I now decided to follow its course across sheet after sheet of the maps in the *Atlas*, using a ruler and inking it in as I went.

During its course through England Two Degrees West traversed at least eleven counties, or parts of them, eight large moors in Yorkshire, something like twenty-seven rivers and innumerable streams. Four hundred and ten miles as the crow flies to the Channel from Berwick-on-Tweed. It didn't sound much.

I considered other options. The Greenwich Meridian would have been a much more famous alternative, but unfortunately on land it lacks staying power. It emerges from the North Sea at Tunstall, north of Withernsea in East Yorkshire, having travelled underwater all the way from the North Pole. Thereafter it goes through ideal biking country unless there is a headwind, and after crossing the Thames at Greenwich drops into the sea at Peacehaven, between Brighton and Newhaven, then comes ashore again at Villers-sur-Mer near Deauville – 'invigorating walk along the sea wall' according to Hachette's *Guide*.

I also wondered what would happen if I started in the extreme north of Scotland and followed Four Degrees West. The answer was that for a lot of the way I would be losing it underwater: in the Dornoch and Moray Firths, in an enormous stretch of the Irish Sea between the mouth of the Solway Firth and Conway Bay (between Llandudno and Anglesey), in the Bristol Channel between Mumbles head in Glamorganshire and the cliffs east of Ilfracombe at Heddon's Mouth, finally saying goodbye to it in Bigbury Bay, South Devon, on the shores of the English Channel.

What one needs for a trip on Four Degrees West is a steamer. Three Degrees West starts on the north coast of Caithness. It then crosses the mouth of the Dornoch Firth and the Moray Firth, then climbs the highest of the Cairngorms and burrows through Dundee. After this it crosses the Firth of Tay, the Firth of Forth and the Border at Canonbie. From Canonbie it heads for the Lake District, Morecambe Bay, Fleetwood, Blackpool, Southport, Liverpool, Birkenhead, the Long Mynd, the Clun and Radnor Forests, the eastern edge of the Black Mountains, Newport, the Severn Estuary, the Bristol Channel off Weston-super-Mare, Sedgemoor, the edge of the Blackdown Hills, and finally leaps into the Channel over Beer Head in Devon, between Lyme Regis and Sidmouth.

For quite some time – about two days – after having 'discovered' Two Degrees West, in what I soon realized were my more Mr Toad-like moments, I seriously considered doing the whole thing on foot, the only way it can be done if you want to stick to the entire route.

I even began laying down a set of rules about what would be permitted in the way of divergences from the meridian. Towns and cities, even large villages through which it passed, would present almost impossible problems. In my wilder imaginings I visualized myself trying to maintain the alignment in Berwick-on-Tweed, scaling garden walls and crunching my way through the English equivalents of Mr McGregor's cucumber frames in nearby Scotland a couple of miles or so further up the coast. Even worse was the prospect of having to scale the city walls, for Berwick is a walled city, hiring a fishing boat to cross the Tweed, only to be confronted by yet more walled gardens, more cucumber frames in Tweedmouth.

In Birmingham it was extremely unlikely that any of the canals would run on the same course as Two Degrees West for more than a few hundred yards. I could see myself entering the backyards of red-brick terrace houses where the privies had been half a century ago, and probably still were in some of them for all I knew, then clumping through the kitchen in my great boots, knocking the tea mugs off the table with my enormous pack, tipping my cap to whoever happened to be watching telly. Probably a Midland version of Alf Garnett, glowering at me from the depths of an armchair with broken springs, whereas I would be mumbling something about 'sorry for the disturbance, trying to catch a train', before emerging in the street through the front door and banging on the front door of the house opposite, where I would begin the whole process again, but this time in reverse.

It was only when I began to study the larger-scale Ordnance Survey maps and was able to gain a more close-up view of all the rivers, streams, torrents and rivulets running through thousands of acres of moorland and all strung out across the route (and a large part of England north of Birmingham is just that) that I realized that it was going to be impossible for someone who was *nicht so jung* to do it on foot, that is unless I had months of summertime at my disposal.

The trouble with Two Degrees West, or any other meridian for that matter, was that it was no use attributing human feelings to it, although I was already in danger of doing just this. It didn't have to eat, or drink, or find somewhere to spend the night. It couldn't even get lost. In fact one of the reasons for its existence, in association with the lines of latitude, was to help people not to do so.

It was the rivers which Two Degrees West crossed with such maddeningly effortless ease that were the real problem for a walker, or a cyclist for that matter. They could quite easily necessitate a detour of five miles or more to the nearest bridge or crossing place. A total of ten miles before one could get back on the route, half a day's walk in winter daylight in November. And where could one find anywhere to stay in winter in such wilderness?

So I decided that I would not become a slave to Two Degrees West, or any other meridian. If I did, I would very soon find myself referring to it as him or her and offering up oblations, rather like a Hindu, perhaps even slaughtering a goat. I wasn't trying for a place in *The Guinness Book of Records* as the man who smashed more cucumber frames than any other on his way from Berwick-on-Tweed to Dancing Ledge. Anyway, I was pretty sure that lots of people had walked from the Scots Border on the A1 to Dorset or somewhere similar, and thousands must have cycled it. The only way to break my dependence on this meridian was by following it when I could and otherwise staying as close to it as possible. And I didn't expect to learn anything significant about the state of England while participating in this trip. In my experience if I start asking people what they think about the state of England they say, 'Sorry, but I've got a train to catch!' Visually, I thought it might be wonderful, at least I hoped so.

In fact the only way for me to do this trip, as I had really known all along, was on a bicycle.

As Wanda had issued an absolute prohibition against my making the journey alone – in fact I was secretly very relieved that she had done so – the next step was to find someone rash enough and fit enough to come with me, on what would be a pretty horrible journey if it rained or snowed. When it came to it, there were only three people I knew well enough to ask. There was Pat Allen, with whom I had cycled from Rotterdam to Dijon. But he had already arranged to go to Spain, so that was that.

There was my grandson, Joseph. Joseph was sixteen, a keen cyclist, and, like Pat, very good with complex machinery. Together with Pat the three of us had made some long excursions along the sea walls on the Suffolk marshes. Unfortunately he was out of the running, too, as he had examinations.

The third contender was Rupert Cotterell, the younger son of some great friends of ours who lived a little way up the valley from where we were in Purbeck. He had just come down from Oxford, having got a degree in Architectural History. A boy of boundless enthusiasm and *joie de vivre*, he looked a bit like Biggles, the intrepid pilot. In fact, while at the university, he had learned to fly and only recently he had zoomed low over the chimney pots of his home in Dorset, scaring his mother near to death. He was also a very good shot, which might come in useful if we ran short of food. Like everyone else of his age in England in 1991, he was having the greatest difficulty in getting a job. He volunteered with alacrity.

The most important thing was to get Rupert a suitable bike without having to buy one. Wanda still had the one she had used in Ireland, the high-tech Overbury Wildcat mountain bike, but it had been made for her and was too small for someone such as Rupert who was more than six feet high. Eventually I borrowed the mountain bike I had used in Ireland from my son-in-law, which I had sold to him, the Overbury Fell Rider. I myself now had the bike that had come made-to-measure from Charles Roberts' workshop in Croydon when Pat Allen and I cycled along the canals.

Theoretically, we weren't going to have to spend very much on the Berwick-on-Tweed–Dorset run. I already had all the panniers and tools which had been assembled for the Irish journey, but both bikes needed expensive new axles and, after finding out the difficulties British Rail was prepared to put in the way of anyone foolish enough to take a couple of bikes from Dorset to Berwick-on-Tweed by train, I decided to hire a van.

We eventually arrived in Berwick-on-Tweed from Edinburgh, where we had restored the van to the rental firm. Armed with five informative pamphlets produced by the Berwick-on-Tweed Civic Society at 20p each – not many free hand-outs here, or at the majority of information offices en route – we 'did' the place that evening. That is to say, we staggered around one and a half miles of ramparts, some of them made of earth and covered with grass, others built of masonry, while the rain fell in torrents and a force 9 gale blew from the east-south-east. This created a boiling sea where it met the ebb in the mouth of the Tweed.

Up there on the walls we were at roof level with the houses in the streets below, where Two Degrees West clove through them before burrowing under the river. With the street lights shining on the wet cobbles in the downpour and mysterious stone staircases leading down into the town, it was rather like being on the set of a Tudor version of *Singin' in the Rain*, which would have had Gene Kelly tapping his way through it dressed in armour.

'*Berwick-on-Tweed* (pr. berrick; officially "upon")', as Baedeker put it in what is almost certainly its last ever guide to Great Britain in the old mould,* is a picturesque place, beautiful when seen from one of the bridges, or from the far bank of the Tweed. One writer† compared it to 'a seventeenth-century engraving of some snug, trim Dutch port'. With its austere, grey stone eighteenth- and nineteenth-century houses and red pantiles, which any demolition man would give his eye teeth to have, its three remarkable bridges, one of them reinforced concrete, its early eighteenth-century barracks, possibly the work of Vanbrugh, and one of the only two Anglican churches built in Britain during the Commonwealth, it is a town very much out of the ordinary; but it is its walls and its situation high above the river and the sea that really make Berwick such a memorable place.

The walls were built in several stages. They were begun in 1296 when Edward I first took the town from the Scots, at which time they consisted of earthern ramparts. The most modern ones were ordered by Elizabeth I,‡ and were built between 1558 and 1569 in anticipation of a joint Scottish/French invasion of England, at the time when Mary Queen of Scots was claimant to the English throne. Between 10 and 12 feet thick and 22 feet high and with five bastions, they were designed by two Italian engineers, Portinari and Jacopo a Contio. In their day they represented the most advanced form of post-medieval military architecture in existence. They cost more than the entire defence budget of England at that time, so much that work on them was suspended in 1569 and never resumed.

Berwick's walls were never besieged. Perhaps it was just as well. Contio and Portinari had equipped them with what are known in military parlance as flankers, recesses with guns mounted in them that allowed flanking fire along the curtain walls between bastion and flanking bastion, a system which always seemed to me a unique opportunity for the

---

* *Northern England*, vol. III, 1970.
† Thomas Sharp in the *Shell Guide to Northumberland*, 1969.
‡ Pevsner says they were built during the reign of Mary Tudor in 1555.

defenders to blow one another to pieces. In fact these flankers were protected by screen walls and were accessible by tunnels. These fortifications were not dismantled until 1819 and had formidable fire power.

The slightest acquaintance with the history of Berwick-on-Tweed makes it sound, so far as the inhabitants are concerned, rather like being condemned to live on the Khyber Pass. Endless feuds and blood-letting led to people shutting themselves up for years in watch towers, afraid to emerge in case they got drilled through the head by an arrow or a bullet.

Founded by the Saxons – its name *Bere Wic* is said to signify 'Grain Port' – it was attacked incessantly and enthusiastically by Picts and Danes. In the eleventh century it was also plundered by mercenaries employed by William the Conqueror. Subsequently, it became the chief seaport of Scotland. In 1214 King John, on his way home after a raid into Scotland, had it burned to the ground, himself applying the first torch to the house in which he had been put up for the night, a severe way to deal with a B. & B. however much lacking in amenity.

Almost everything older than the Elizabethan walls has been swept away in the course of the seemingly endless series of bloody, mindless encounters. And this tradition of destruction has continued into modern times. Even the castle, a rather important one historically, was knocked down to allow for the construction of the railway station on its site and a number of old buildings more recently bit the dust in order to make room for a hideous bus station.

Its greatest period of prosperity was in the reign of King Alexander XI of Scotland. He succeeded to the throne at the age of eight, being placed on the coronation stone at Scone in the presence of seven lords, seven bishops and a great concourse of people, and died in 1286 as a result of falling over a cliff.

At four o'clock on an afternoon in mid-November, Rupert and I stood on the cliffs on the northern outskirts of Berwick-on-Tweed. Now, for the first time, we were actually on our bikes. Our baggage had been left in our nearby B. & B. It was cold. Our breath smoked picturesquely. There was not a breath of wind, or a single cloud in the sky. The sun was already setting. And I was confronted by my first hole, at the very start of the whole thing.

'Brotherston's Hole,' Rupert said in an assumed Northumbrian accent which I was unable to emulate, heavy with disbelief. 'If this is Brotherston's Hole, it's very disappointing.'

As Brotherston's Hole marked the beginning of our journey along Two Degrees West it was important to locate it before setting off for the south as otherwise we wouldn't have seen the place where our journey began.

We had been directed to this particular bit of cliff by a local man. The one inch Ordnance Survey map of the area, now long out of date, showed that the Hole was near a firing range and on a golf course, but what this man had thought at a distance was a firing range was actually a bunker on a golf course. After giving out this misleading information he had moved off smartly. Now there was no one to ask.

What we were now looking at could scarcely be described as a hole, except in the critical sense of the word, in which case it could equally well have been described as a dump.

There were a couple of sandstone promontories with a beach between them, overlooked by a holiday village full of caravans, a paddling pool, a playground and, on the particular promontory on which we were currently standing, a ladies' and gents' convenience. Most of these amenities were finished in colours which clashed with the green grass of the golf course and other items of nature. And out beyond the foreshore was the North Sea, what used to be known as the German Ocean, dead flat, drained of colour at this hour of day, and very, very sad.

The view was much more inspiring immediately inland, where the complex ramparts of Berwick-on-Tweed with fine, leafless trees, churches and various secular buildings rising above them were silhouetted against the setting sun. Fortunately, at this moment, a man of about fifty appeared, mounted on an over-sized, rather rude-looking horse.

'Brotherston's Hole,' he said in the incredulous tone of voice that local inhabitants invariably reserve for visitors (otherwise loonies), at the same time dismounting from his giant steed. 'Do you mean the Gully? You're miles out for the Gully. Why, it's up there, half way to Scotland.'

'But Scotland's only three miles from here, isn't it?' Rupert said, impetuous youth, earning himself a withering glance.

'Well, that's what I said, a mile and a half,' said the horseman, a trifle testily, on account of having to deal with a couple of *dummkopfen* on the shores of the German Ocean on which he probably thought we had landed clandestinely by *falt boot* (collapsible boat).

'You can follow the coast path,' he continued, more kindly now, 'but you'd best get on your bikes, go back to the town, take the A1 for Edinburgh, turn right when you get to the housing estate, then cross the railway and the golf course to the cliffs. That's where the Gully is. And you'd better get a move on, otherwise it'll be dark.'

In spite of this admonition we got him to take a flash picture of the two of us with the convenience in the background in case he was wrong and this was the site of Brotherston's Hole for, as Rupert said, when he was out of earshot, thundering away on his great horse like something out of Scott's *Marmion*, 'You can't be too careful when starting on a journey and we might not pass this way again,' something I had already vowed not to do as far as this particular holiday resort was concerned.

Then we got back on our bikes, stormed back up along the perimeter walls, took a right on to the main road for Scotland, zoomed off down through the housing estate, crossed a bridge over the main railway line, and on to one of the fairways of the golf course we had already been frequenting, or perhaps it was another one.

'I say,' said Rupert, looking decidedly Bigglesish in his biking crash helmet and long, lemon-coloured scarf, 'we can't ride on the goff-course, it wouldn't be right.' A keen golfer, he calls it 'goff'.

I had a crash helmet, too, but Rupert's mum had covered his with a bit of fine Border tweed which made his look less environmentally intrusive than mine did.

'We don't have to ride on the greens,' I said, 'only across the fairways. We don't want to come all the way back here tomorrow, just to see a hole, that is if there is one.' And I took off without waiting to find out how Rupert was going to solve this particular problem of conscience about whether it was possible to ride a bike across a fairway and still continue to be a keen 'goffer'.

The Hole, an undeniable Hole, but not a very large one, was a tiny sandstone cove below steep cliffs, in which the sea was sucking horribly in the caves at shore level. It was exactly the sort of place where I expected Two Degrees West to writhe up, like a huge worm or sea serpent, and start crawling off across the golf course in the direction of Berwick-on-Tweed and Dancing Ledge.

It also turned out to form a terrible impediment to a golfer's sanity, being exactly in the middle of the 57-yard long eighth hole, rendering bunkers superfluous. In fact two young men were already half way down the sides of whatever it was, trying to find their golf balls which had both fallen into it when they had attempted to whack them across the chasm.

'Par Four, very hard to play,' one of them said in answer to Rupert's enquiry as to what it was like, Rupert having just come sprinting down from the railway line where he had locked his bike to a fence. 'And bloody expensive in balls,' the other one said, now almost invisible down below, still digging away with a club in the vegetation with no success.

Neither of them had heard of Brotherston's Hole. Just as the horseman had, they called it the Gully. Perhaps it wasn't Brotherston's Hole, although a bit of what might have been a firing range was still visible, although it, too, could have been a bunker. Perhaps there is no such thing as Brotherston's Hole. Perhaps it is a figment of the imagination of some crazy Ordnance Surveyor, named Brotherston.

The morning after our attempt to discover the 'real' Brotherston's Hole we set off from Berwick-on-Tweed to pursue our journey on Two Degrees West. Scarcely had we done so than a sign indicating the route to Holy Island sprang into view, tempting us away from the Devil's Causeway, which undoubtedly ran along Two Degrees West. In this way we wasted – if one can call a visit to Holy Island a waste of time – the greater part of the day and the lesser part of a night.

We then found ourselves in the darkness at Wooler, a town picturesquely situated on the River Till in Northumberland. Two Degrees West simply abandoned us here and took off to the south-east in the direction of Morpeth, which is almost in the North Sea, leaving us to flounder in a labyrinth of lanes on the eastern flanks of the Cheviot Hills. Now, for the first time, we both realized that we were not in control of our destinies when travelling with Two Degrees West. The route (we had very little chance of modifying it) took us through the Roxburgh Forest – I won't attempt a description of it as one forest, especially a coniferous one, is very similar to another.

Next east of Redesdale to cross the Roman Wall east of Hexham, and then over the Tyne. Most of the river crossings on this trip turned out to be eastward ones – this was no exception.

We crossed the Derwent, which rises at the northern end of the Pennines. Then we came to Weardale, Teesdale, Swaledale, Wensleydale, Wharfedale and Airedale, south-east of Skipton, and a river I can find on a map but not identify, between Burnley and Bradford. By this time we were both beginning to be a bit tired of dales and cycling uphill – we had long since started sending home items no longer wanted: maps, guide books, used clothing, etc.

Then round, not over, Bleaklow Hill (2,060 feet), across the River Colne, east of Rochdale; and afterwards west of Kinder Scout to travel down the eastern side of Manchester. Meanwhile the weather did everything it is capable of in Britain. It hailed and snowed in blizzards, and rained in torrents. And sometimes it seemed to us, churning away on our triple chainwheels for ten miles or so uphill, unnaturally hot. We eventually arrived in Buxton in the middle of the night and the following day we cycled alongside a canal to Stoke-on-Trent.

Once we had crossed the Roman Wall we began to have trouble with thorns, which now intensified. North of the Roman Wall the fields were divided from each other by drystone walls, with hardly any thorns to worry about, but between Stoke-on-Trent and the Dorset border we suffered more than fifty punctures. It was the time of year when farmers in middle and southern England trimmed their thorn hedges, leaving millions of thorns on the waysides and the banks of the canals, canals we had intended to make use of to avoid the hills. There were so many thorns that at one point it seemed that we might have to abandon the journey altogether. Every time we got a puncture we had to turn the bicycle upside down to get the wheel, or wheels, off, and this meant removing the pannier-bags too. Sometimes the tyres on both bikes punctured at the same time, and we often cried, literally, from sheer vexation. Once all four tyres punctured simultaneously.

It eventually proved impossible to mend all the holes using puncture repair kits and we had to buy new inner tubes. By the time we found out that it was possible to buy puncture-proof bands to insert between the inner tube and the tyre it was too late to find any.

After riding through Cannock Chase where there is a German war cemetery, Two Degrees West took us bang through the middle of Birmingham, then across the Vale of Gloucester, across the Valley of the Upper Thames (visiting the alleged source of it, near Cirencester (which was dry), the Cotswolds, the Vale of Malmesbury, the Marlborough Downs and Salisbury Plain. Beautiful cycling country.

On Salisbury Plain we called a temporary halt in order to visit a small but rather beautiful church on the edge of a small village. On the opposite side of the road to it there was a very attractive small country house built of flint and brick – the sort of place the owners might ask a million or more for and not be disappointed.

The entrance to the front of the house was through a white gate. We decided to leave the bikes propped against the entrance wall as there was no provision on the other side of the main road for parking anything. Rupert chose a place which was slightly more conspicuous than the one I had chosen for my own bike.

As we turned to cross the road the front door opened and a man wearing a dark-blue pullover with 'Police' embroidered on it appeared. He was armed with a Smith and Wesson in a shoulder holster and had a mobile phone.

'Excuse me, Sir,' he said to Rupert in very polite, rather epicene tones. 'Your bicycle, Sir, is rather in our field of vision. Could you possibly move it? Just a few feet, Sir.' And he began to turn away. For the first time I noticed that this Jane Eyreish house had a radio mast sprouting from the top of it.

'I say,' said Rupert, 'is this a Safe House?'

'As a matter of fact it is, Sir,' the policeman said.

Then, made happy by this brief encounter with such a special sort of policeman, we rode up over Grovely Ridge where the local inhabitants used to sing the praises – one hopes they still do – of the great woods of Grovely, and descended into the Vale of Wardour. After which we repaired our last puncture of the season on the lawn of a friend in the depths of Cranborne Chase, between Salisbury and Blandford.

The most frightening part of the entire journey was crossing Poole Harbour on Two Degrees West to the Isle of Purbeck in a small rowing boat propelled by a kindly fisherman with the bikes slung around our necks, ready to take us plummeting to the bottom if we capsized.

By now we had covered about 490 miles, according to our meters, which didn't seem very much; and had been on the road for about a fortnight. It seemed longer.

The last bit by bike was to Langton Matravers; we then went down on foot through the disused quarry workings to Dancing Ledge, a great slab of Purbeck stone on which the waves break furiously in heavy weather. The Ledge was invisible when we got there, as it had been quite dark for some time.

And at last home to West Bucknowle, to find Wanda waiting for us under a triumphal arch with 'Welcome' inscribed on it, dressed as a maid and pouring us Champagne.

We were glad to be back in Dorset. One gets tired of bed-and-breakfasts, however good they may be.

In Calabria

ONE MORNING in the early 1990s we arrived in Gioia Tauro in Calabria, a part of Italy we had always wanted to see after looking at Edward Lear's splendid lithograph drawings reproduced in his *Journals of a Landscape Painter in Southern Calabria and the Kingdom of Naples*, published in 1852.

The modern parts of Gioia Tauro were places of nightmare, overflowing with motor car repair shops and vendors of spare parts. On one side of a street there was a hecatomb of dead vehicles with piles of millstones on top of them, presumably to prevent them blowing away. Here, we breakfasted on coffee and slightly dusty *occhi di bue*, delicious pastries with a blob of red jam in the middle, hence the name, bull's eyes.

We left Gioia Tauro by way of immense olive groves. There were splendid views over Scilla, partner of Charybdis, on the Sicilian side of the Strait of Messina – almost exactly, except that now the sea was rough, as Lear depicted it when he was there in the autumn of 1847. Now white chestnuts were in flower and there was orange blossom everywhere. Here, in Calabria, the wild flowers have a life-span in spring of about three weeks.

We failed to make the turning off the *autostrada* on to route 106 and had to go back some miles in order to do so. Here, every available ridge facing seawards was clothed in houses, most of them no more than grey, concrete shells, unfinished because their owners either lacked planning permission, or the means to bribe the local authorities.

The first part of the 106 was built up as far as Pellaro, and the railway line runs along the coast between the main road and the sea, all the way to Taranto, making access to the beaches difficult. These were mostly gravel and rather squalid. Palms and prickly pears flourished, making the wearing of nothing but a bathing costume hazardous. At Fornace Lazzaro Saline Ioniche, as a signpost had it – could this be one place? – there was a huge chemical plant with tall, striped chimneys, condemned and out of action. There were piles of wind-blown plastic everywhere and dry river beds full of assorted muck. We had long since begun to wish that we hadn't come. At San Melito di Porto Salvo, the southernmost point of Italy, you can't even see the sea. But the smell of orange blossom was everywhere and there were great displays of geraniums on the balconies of the houses on every hand.

We drove to Pentedattilo, an inland village. Immediately you leave the coast you are in another, better-for-the-traveller world, because no one can afford to live so far from everywhere unless he or she is an old-age pensioner. Here, in this lonely valley of the San Elia there were uncountable numbers of yellow daisies growing in the now abandoned fields; and there was broom in flower and millions of industrious bees burring away.

Altogether six families lived in the village and at the far end of it there was a huge rock. What Norman Douglas, in his splendid book *Old Calabria*, described as 'a molar turned upside down, with its fangs in the air', which made me feel that he was trying too hard.

Among the inhabitants were Signor Francesco Roda and his wife, formerly of the Ristorante Montebello, in Toronto. They were both born in Pentedattilo, emigrated to Canada, lived there for twenty years and returned recently to spend the rest of their lives in this lovely but lonely place. Now they were putting their minute house at the end of the village in order.

Back to Melito on the coast in search of food, in another world. This was Monday and most restaurants were shut at this time of year. Eventually we found one which fed us on *calamare* and pasta. On leaving it we found that the hydraulic system of what was our brand-new Citroën was leaking. We took it to a garage in Melito without result. It had to be a Citroën garage, because only it would have the parts. We then drove to a Citroën garage on the outskirts of Reggio Calabria. They claimed to have solved the problem, but they hadn't. Then back to Melito, of which we were beginning to tire. How one began to envy Lear with his pack animals. Here the *autostrada*, or whatever it was, came to an end in an impressive chaos of concrete, not because the authorities had run out of money to complete it but because some savant discovered an ancient city buried astride the route which had to be excavated first.

And then to Palizzi by a winding road above the deep gorge of a river of the same name. The whole valley was a paradise of flowers such as we had rarely seen – daisies, yellow and white, violets, anchusa, a hairy-stemmed plant with a blue flower, broom and a yellow flower that can express a poisonous milk. On the way we passed a house, one of the few not in ruins, where a small boy on horseback was being led by his grandfather on a rein. There were goats in a pen, and a pig on the loose, and two ladies, mother and daughter, who later, when we stopped to talk to them on the way back, turned out to be very nice and jolly. They had heard of Inghilterra, but only recently. They had no TV.

Then, suddenly, we were in sight of the astonishing panorama of Palizzi, just as Lear saw it in August 1847, overhung by a colossal rock; and we went down into the village, into the main street at the foot of the rock, which at that time of the day, just before dusk, was full of local inhabitants who seemed both surprised and pleased to see us. And there, in a dark shop, we drank dark red wine, served to us by a lady dressed in black, which was extremely good. Once, she said, Palizzi had had 900 inhabitants, now it had 600. Many had gone away to work but they mostly came back at Christmas and Easter, or to retire here and eventually die. Another, much older lady, also dressed in widow's black, identified the house in which she lived, which could be seen in Lear's picture near the bridge. There was not a hope of finding any accommodation here, or in the next village higher up, Pietrapenaata (630m), which had only about 120 people in it – no restaurants and no rooms, either. So back to Palizzi Marina, where we found a place to stay.

The hotel of Giordano Domenico – modern, bare but run by kindly people – was OK. Signor Giordano gave Wanda some *fave* (green beans) to eat raw. What, she asked me, could she do with them? She was filled in with *fave*. How do you dispose of a large handful of them in an hotel? They won't flush down the loo – not in this hotel, anyway – and you have to produce the skins as evidence of having eaten them. Eventually I crept out of the hotel and threw them in the sea.

In the Citroën, the hydraulic system was still leaking, but the men at the local garage said it was only overflow. But why should it overflow?

The view from our room was not inspiring. Across the road there were some plastic sheds, and what looked like a plastic oven. There was also, facing the 106, a bashed-up-looking house, which had lost part of its roof. Every so often a train passed, drawn by engines fitted with piercing whistles, just as if Chirico was in charge. And beyond all this, a sad, lifeless sea. We were some pickers, coming voluntarily to Calabria in April.

The main street led up to a church with a sign over it telling us to join the Labour Party. We made various plans, all of them abortive, as to how we might stay in Palizzi in the mountains. One of the more fantastic was that Domenico would send up a load of mattresses for us to recline on; but then it transpired that there was no open space in Palizzi large enough on which to open them up. Dinner was pasta and red mullet, cooked by the young man who had caught them. There was red and white wine, both rather good.

We stopped at S. Pasquale di Bova Marina where we met a 77-year-old Greek, who obliged us with a few Greek phrases. Then we went on to Bova in pouring rain. Of Bova Lear wrote: 'The great characteristic of Calabrian towns, picturesquely speaking, appears to consist in the utter irregularity of their design, the houses being built on, and among separate masses of rock, as if it had been intended to make them look as much like natural bits of scenery as possible.' The Marzano Palazzo, to which Lear had been invited, 'is the most prominent of the houses here, and, homely and unornamented as it is, stands on its brown crag, looking over worlds of blue wood, and Sicily floating on the horizon's edge, with a most imposing grandeur – and just where a painter would have put it.' Well, there were no islands floating in grandeur on this particular morning with visibility down to about a hundred feet. We felt lucky to be able to see our shoes.

Bova was built along the flanks of an enormous rock. It had 800 inhabitants of whom fifty spoke a Greek dialect. They were all extremely friendly, as they were when Lear visited the place in July 1847. We climbed up to the rock through deserted lanes, and there, in a shop with a sign outside which announced *Kalo Irtete*, Calabrian Greeks were drinking excellent red wine.

Here, on the premises, we met the Mayor who in turn introduced us to a very handsome man of seventy-six [with an impressive moustache] who taught the dialect. Efforts were also being made to make the young speak modern Greek. Here, too, we met another old man who carried his entire Second World War military record around with him on a single, torn envelope. He gave it to us to admire but we were terrified that it might disintegrate, as it was blowing half a gale.

In the piazza there was an enormous railway engine, parked there, but with no rails to run on. And there was an astonishing collection of palaces, including Lear's Palazzo Marzano, and churches, about a dozen in all, and the Cathedral, the Chiesa di S. Maria Theotoca, that had been refurbished after 1783.

From Bova we climbed through very lonely, almost uninhabited country and saw the poisonous yellow flower locally known as *tasso*. Here, if the map is correct, you could walk thirty to forty kilometres from east to west – or the other way round – without encountering a road or a village; but roads may have been bulldozed since that time. Here we saw three wild pigs and two large piglets, one black and one brown, and a cream sow, all galloping about, thoroughly enjoying themselves.

But the sound and feel of heavy rain in these dense woods and of the River Amendolea far below induced a feeling of indescribable melancholy. There was also a cuckoo, and a lot of sheep banging their bells, and huge supplies of the poisonous *tasso*. What more could we want?

We came to Ghorio di Roghudi, Greek for 'of the rocks', a large village almost completely dead. Everywhere there were disused cars twenty years old, some with trees and other vegetation growing up out of them. And there was an abandoned post office and thousands of broken bottles, as if the inhabitants had had a battle before leaving, and whole cellars silted up with plastic sheets and bags. But a field of broad beans and lettuce growing in the rich, red earth showed that someone was working the land, if not living there. Then in a little piazza we saw two strange-looking women, one of them with white hair cascading over her shoulders, gazing down on us from one of the rooftops but making no sign of recognition that we were there. Nearby there was a child's bike, abandoned for ever. And there was a little church with a pyramidal spire. The houses were all locked. We saw a doll impaled with a nail on a tree, which was rather disturbing, and a solitary tethered lamb, guarded by a ferocious tethered dog.

The narrow, cobbled lanes were choked with rubbish. We saw a white cat with ginger ears. Finally, we met another human being, the man who still cultivated the field we had already seen. He was between fifty and sixty and lived alone. His house was without electric light, he said. He spoke Italian and old Greek. We couldn't find out where he lived; he was rather reticent about it. Anyway we didn't get invited. Here, he said, there used to be *intagliatori e tessitrici*, carvers of kitchen utensils, sweet moulds and so on with traditional Greek motifs. They were also famous for weaving *ginestra* (broom) in Greco-Byzantine designs, and they made cheese moulds; their pecorino and goat cheeses were famous.

After all this to Roghudi Vecchia. The village, one of the shepherds who now inhabited it told us, was finally abandoned in 1971.

Why did they abandon their cars, the inhabitants of these and other villages? Did they take what for them must have been the great leap forward into the modern, industrial world, or is there still some place where they can practise their skills?

We then reached Roccaforte del Greco, one of the four communes making up the Communità Grecanica, by a wild road lined with yet more abandoned cars and lorries. And there was even a garage with a tree growing through its roof. At the Chiesa dei Tripepi di Boya, a church of Byzantine inspiration, there were the remains of a tower, and the Virgin and Child in what looked like a telephone box. And in the floor was an open burial vault. Here the Greek dialect has persisted more than anywhere else.

Then on and up to Iermanata, which must be one of the loneliest inhabited places in all Italy. Five families lived there – there were no shops or houses, only stone bothies. All of them, they said, were related to one another. One of the goatherds, a boy of sixteen, told us that none of them wanted to go down to live at Palizzi Marina.

Inside one of the bothies the owners had very modern, shiny, up-to-date black bentwood furniture. In it we were offered strong red wine from a Veuve Clicquot bottle. The room of one of the little girls, the youngest, had 'I love you' written on the door in English. The mother, dark, thin and attractive, a Veuve herself, wanted us to stay. We should have done.

From Palizzi Marina, in watery sunshine we drove forty kilometres eastward to Ardore Marina, and then inland up a broad valley to Bombile, to visit the Santuario della Madonna della Grotta. There, an old lady in black went off to get the enormous key to the place, in exchange for which I gave her my passport. The church was about a couple of kilometres beyond the village on the eastern side of a deep valley, reached through orange groves.

It was built inside a cavern excavated in the pale, cream-coloured tufa and had a pretty façade and a baroque doorway dated 1758. Inside it was rather like being in a tent pitched in a cave. The statue of the venerated Madonna was visited by 10,000 pilgrims on 1 May. The waxen ex-votos and spooky waxen heads were modern additions.

To Locri, on the coast, in search of food – this is no *route des gastronomes* – and somewhere to sleep. It was a really awful place. So we moved on to Siderno Marina, nearby, nicer than Locri but almost literally bursting at the seams with locals doing the *passeggiata* in motor cars, driving up and down the main street, or casing the window stock of the best jeweller in town, who does a roaring trade in Rolexes hewn from solid nuggets of gold. And all the shops were doing a roaring trade at 9 p.m. In Siderno, no on ever goes to bed.

Eventually we chose the Aster Hotel – was this a misprint for Astor? We tried to imagine real Astors living in this terrain but had to give up. The choice of *trattorie* was more difficult – but it was important we were only getting one square meal a day. Passers-by in the street when asked which they would choose said the important thing was to choose one with a woman cook, and for this reason we ended up in the Futa Francesco. Unfortunately the old mother of the cook recognized some truffle-like objects which we had been given at the bothy in Iermenata as something that you fried. A serious mistake if they really were truffles and only needed to be grated over whatever was being prepared, rice or whatever; but we didn't think they were truffles – wrong time of year.

The next morning we were awoken by a mad pealing of bells which made us think that the Saracens were landing, and a workman armed with a hammer appeared to be knocking the building down. Aster/Astor would not have enjoyed this, or what the old lady did to the so-called truffles.

Worse, the Citroën's hydraulics were still leaking. So we drove back to the garage in Locri, which wasn't really far, just a bore. One side of the vehicle was now thickly coated with hydraulic oil. Citroën at Locri claimed to have cured the trouble, but they hadn't. From Locri – may it sink into the sea! – to Gerace. It was now warm and sunny for the first time on this crazy trip. A winding road with vineyards and olives and one enormous wisteria tree eventually deposited us in an open space near the castle. Then down under a high archway into a stone-flagged, assymetrical square overlooked by the Cathedral, which was shut. Outside in the square the Bar Cattedrale was very old outside, very new inside with more of the black bentwood furniture, and there were some old shops with no goods for sale in view, and there was a palazzo with a large rusticated arch, lacking its capstone, which lent an air of instability to the scene. At the Bar Alimentari in Via Zalenco the proprietor sold us excellent red wine at 3,200 lire a litre. In this street in which the houses were mostly pebble-dashed, lemon trees, wild roses, vines and geraniums flourished. On the upper storeys there were bulbous iron balconies. Here, in the eighteenth century, there were more than sixty churches, eight convents and numerous monasteries. The Cathedral was opened for us by a boy. The way into it led through the crypt, its roof supported by a forest of columns – actually twenty-six. In it the Capella della Madonna dell' Itriance displayed a painting believed to have arrived miraculously from Constantinople. Then up a flight of worn steps into the largest church in Calabria, built in the time of the Swabians, consecrated in 1045 and restored after an earthquake in the eighteenth century, the nave and aisles supported by a further twenty granite and marble columns. After a big Saracenic raid on Locri, a sparrow hawk led the survivors to this place, and when the Saracens came again in 901 they found Gerace too heavily fortified for them.

In brilliant sunshine Wanda produced a delicious meal on the acropolis, the Piazza Tribuna, next to the Castle, which is separated from the rock by a deep moat – fried eggs, tomatoes and strawberries. Then a hundred schoolchildren descended on the place to eat their picnics, just like us, and played for an hour and a half. The only hotel was closed because the joint owners had had a row; the restaurant was closed because it was a Monday. In search of food for our evening meal we drove miles to a place called Passo di Ropola, having passed on the way a big road block manned by soldiers and Carabinieri – a bank had just been robbed. The Passo was high up under Monte San Iunio, where there was a restaurant. A notice outside said that they served only parties of ten, but a relative, hovering about, said that if we left a letter saying that we wanted dinner it would be cooked. So we did.

Down to Gerace Inferiore. The Capuchin monastery there has a nice baroque façade. It was abandoned forty years previously. Now the church, chapels, cloisters, refectories were all collapsing and the cloister garden was a jungle. Everywhere there were crucifixes – the largest was life-size – from which Christ had been taken down, with a real hammer and real nails hanging on the cross-piece. And everywhere other smaller crucifixes, silver-painted candlesticks, candelabra and shattered plaster-of-Paris figures of saints and Neapolitan terracotta figures of saints, were also broken.

The wind had now got up and was very strong, howling through the building, stirring up tracts and other theological literature of anything up to a century ago; and they were carried down the sheer drop outside the building through the broken windows and then, on an up-draught in through the windows, back into the building, like a cloud of white birds. All this because we had left the front door open.

By the time it was dark, we set off for the distant restaurant, where we hoped they were cooking us a dinner, the Trattoria San Filippo. Everything was ready. We ate pasta *capretto* – pasta with very young kid – very strong sausages and very strong local wine. The only other guests were two local boys who were complaining about the activities of the Mafia, without actually ever naming the organization. They were both relatives of the *padrone* – one lived at Salsomaggiore in Provincia Parma to which his family had moved. 'I don't know anything about them,' the other said, 'but I do know that when they come here they leave 20,000 on the plate.'

Way Out in Anatolia

———————— ❦ ————————

SOUTHWARDS FROM ANKARA, that deliberately but improbably sited capital, the E5 traversed the upland steppe of Central Anatolia on its way from Ostend to the Syrian border at Antakya. Trees were few, peasants harvested with tractors or sickles, heroes burnt stubble under an incandescent sky and everything was the colour of ripe corn cobs. July is not the best time for this region, spring when the steppe is green or autumn are better, but one travels when the opportunity presents itself, for it might well not recur.

Three thousand feet up, the road undulated past villages of mud houses with roofs of straw and little groves of apple trees, with the long lines of telegraph poles marching across the landscape parallel to it. In prehistoric times this was a region of forest, the last vestiges of which were destroyed by the Arab invaders in the seventh and eighth centuries. Then the steppe was abandoned – the Turkish nomads from the Ural and Altai mountains found it disagreeable when they reached it in the twelfth century – until Siberian Turks from Tomsk and Tartars from the Caspian finally settled the country westwards and north-westwards of the Tuz Gölü, the Great Salt Lake, in the 1900s.

The road descended into the depression of the Tuz Gölü, a vast shallow salt pan along the lake's eastern shore which expands and contracts under the winter rain and summer sun. In winter it covers more than 600 square miles, about the same area as Hertfordshire. It is a place of mirage, where the escarpments along its shores exhibit an extraordinary range of colours: apricot, yellows and vivid greens.

Now, in the torrid light of mid-afternoon, its waters were pale, almost frozen-looking, with a steamy exhalation hanging over them. Black and brown cattle stood in the shallows, but did not drink. Sheep were flaked out on the still green grass down by the shore, guarded by shepherds who had taken refuge from the appalling sun in little pools of shadow, provided by stooks of straw delicately balanced on sticks.

Parched, we drank *ayran*, yoghurt mixed with water and some salt, at a tea house in Sereflikoçhisar, a little oasis with some new, balconied houses, where the drivers of mammoth lorries, which up to now had been pouring dust over us when they ran on the verges, also took their ease.

It was a pity, we felt, that we had not started from Ankara later in the afternoon. At sunset the waters of the lake would have come alive. A hundred and forty miles from Ankara we turned off eastwards from the E5. Here we were on the frontiers of ancient Cappadocia, a region occupied by, among others, Hittites, Greeks (for a time after the break-up of Alexander's empire it was an independent state with an Iranian nobility), Romans (it was evangelized by Peter), Byzantines, the Seljuks, whose administration finally collapsed in 1304, after lasting 200 years, and Mongols and Ottoman Turks.

Ahead, the summit of Hasan Daği, a 10,000ft extinct volcano, loomed through the haze which completely enveloped its flanks, and in a few minutes we were in Aksaray, a real oasis town on the edge of the semi-desert through which we had passed, with ilex and poplars and willows bowing and shimmering in the evening breeze, on the banks of a river which comes down from another volcano mountain, the Melendiz, one of a chain which in eruption made Cappadocia the unique region it is.

Aksaray was a place of Seljuk mosques, *medreses* (Muslim religious schools), the pointed mausolea called *türbesi*, *hamams*, covered markets, storks' nests, old houses with overhanging upper storeys, masses of new buildings and small boys asking for cigarettes, none of whom seemed to know that each pack bore a Government Health Warning.

Now the Ulu Yol, the Sultan's Road, which linked the Seljuk capital, Konya, with the Seljuk Empire in Persia, climbed eastwards past eroded red cliffs. The sun was sinking rapidly now, setting fire to the water in the irrigation ditches and illuminating the men and women on donkeys and in carts returning from the fields. The men wore drab dark suits and caps; but the women were brilliant. One had a white headdress, a yellow apron and a crimson skirt, another an orange head scarf, a wine-coloured skirt and a bright green apron. All had their faces wrapped, not from modesty, but against the all-pervading dust.

We were among fields of lava now and hills like crumbling sand castles. The few habitations were built of masonry with the texture and colour of *pâté de campagne*. Then, in the last of the light, we came to an enormous, high-walled building constructed from blocks of smooth, wonderfully joined stone, reinforced by buttresses and with towers at the angles. This was the Ağzikarahan, built by the Seljuks in the thirteenth century and one of the finest *hans* in Anatolia, places in which travellers and merchants gathered at night for accommodation and mutual protection against robbers at no cost to themselves. We found the custodian and went through the monumental gateway, which was decorated with stalactites, into a magnificent colonnaded courtyard full of bats.

We went on towards Nevşehir, passing without seeing a lake which, according to Nagel's *Guide to Turkey*, was full of tortoises. Nevşehir was a not very exciting town of salmon- and shrimp-paste-coloured houses among vineyards – it is a good region for wine – with a ruined Ottoman citadel on a hill, a modern hotel with a swimming pool, and a shop which sold rugs and carpets.

We ate in a restaurant near the river, where the wine was cooled under jets of water and a great, captive eagle stood on a post contemplating us gloomily.

We were in the land of canyons and rock settlements; but that evening we were indifferent to them. As always, after a day spent travelling and sightseeing in Anatolia, it was nice to go to bed.

'For the rock churches and settlements it is best to leave at sunrise,' I was told. This is so that one can savour 'the effects' and avoid shambling about in the heat of the day. It is in fact just as good to view them towards evening; but then what do you do in the morning? We did both, holing up in a cave during the mid-afternoon.

On this first morning the driver failed to materialize. During our almost too long acquaintanceship in Anatolia either he or his abominable vehicle were broken down, sometimes simultaneously, and by the time we reached the first site around 9.30, the 'effects' were gone and it was becoming too hot for pleasurable contemplation – it was fine inside the dwellings, the trouble was you had to come out. On the following three mornings we left at cock crow.

Many of the canyons wind down through the lava plateau towards the Kizil Irmak, a river which eventually flows into the Black Sea near Samsun. Here, in remote times it opened out into a considerable lake, and when this finally drained away the land began to erode with the astonishing results that can be seen today, a process which is still going on and with such rapid effect that fears are entertained that the landscape and the habitations in it may literally disappear.

In these valleys, cut off from the Mediterranean by the Taurus Mountains, the indigenous inhabitants took up residence, happily isolated to some extent from the attentions of their own native rulers and enjoying a degree of immunity from invading Hittites, Greeks, Romans, Arabs and nomad hordes, and this remoteness encouraged Christian anchorites and later whole religious communities to settle in them. The soil was good and perennial springs made up for the inadequate rainfall on the plateau itself, enabling the cultivation of wheat, apricots and vines, which are still staple products. What was equally important, the tufa was amazingly soft and so in the improbably coloured rock walls – pale yellow, mauve, bright pink, violet and the black of basalt are some of the shades – these embryonic troglodytes tunnelled away like moles (you can make impressive progress using nothing more than a sharpened stick), constructing labyrinthine villages with olive-pressing rooms, grain mills, stables, store houses, while the devout worked away at hermitages, oratories, churches and entire monastic establishments, adorning them lavishly from about the end of the ninth century with frescoes, some of them superb. And they continued to do so until the thirteenth century, although there are more modern paintings at Sinaso and Galveri where Greek communities survived into the nineteenth century. Altogether some 120 religious structures here and in the Peristrema valley near Aksaray still exist.

The only external evidence of the existence of these wall settlements – except in places where a wall has collapsed exposing the interior excavations like a cut through a gruyère – are the doors and windows, some of them inaccessibly high up because of the continuing erosion of the valley floors, and the mouths of the pigeon houses, brilliantly painted to attract the birds whose droppings are still used to manure the fields and vineyards. At Soğanli, south of Nevşehir, there are thousands of these nesting boxes.

In the first centuries of the Christian era when persecution was a way of life the Cappadocians also engaged in the construction of underground towns and villages. At Kaymakli and Derinkuyu, south of Nevşehir, the present-day villages are made up of conventional cube houses in brilliant whites and blues, around which the inhabitants carry on their harvesting in the immense fields using sickles. Beneath their feet, infinitely more sophisticated, are level upon level of piazzas, dwelling houses, cemeteries and chapels, with their own carefully hidden ventilation systems and well shafts, all sealed off from the outer world in times of trouble by circular stones nearly five feet in diameter, which could be rolled down to block the entrances from within.

The lowest level at Kaymakli – there are seven – is 228 feet below ground, at Derinkuyu 390 feet, and its two towns are linked by a tunnel 5 miles long. At Özkonak, north of the Kizil Irmak, there is another subterranean city, said to be able to accommodate 60,000 people, which sounds improbable. Their use persisted throughout the Arab invasions in the seventh and eighth centuries.

The elements which create the valleys also produce the marvellous *peribacalari*, fairy chimneys. These begin as vertical cracks in the tufa which gradually erode into groups of polygonal blocks. These, in turn, are rounded by rain and wind into isolated, conical pillars, each with a cap of harder material which arrests further erosion until it is dislodged and the final wasting-away begins.

Some of these *peribacalari*, which resemble gigantic phalli or fungi, according to one's state of mind, are sixty feet high. There are thousands of them, and some, too, have become dwellings and churches.

At Avcilar an entire valley is filled with such houses. In the 'Monk's Valley' near Zilve, one of them, used by a hermit, is provided with a frescoed chapel, a bed and pillow hewn from tufa and an inscription to that connoisseur of the uncomfortable, St Simeon Stylites.

Perhaps strangest of all are the really enormous rock masses at Ortahisar and Üçhisar, which tower above the plateau and their respective villages and appear to have been gnawed by over-size rodents.

These are the structures that might have been dreamed of by Gaudi in Barcelona.

After days spent in some of the less frequented of the valleys among the caves and cones and labyrinths and churches in which rank upon rank of wide-eyed, solemn, painted figures look down from walls and domes and apses, it is the outer world which begins to seem unreal. The impossibly dark blue sky overhead, the silence only broken by the somniferous sounds made by the pigeons, with an occasional violent clattering of wings when they explode out of their houses into the open air; the wind sighing in the window openings which also let great shafts of sunlight into what would otherwise be interiors as black as pitch – all conspire to turn one's thoughts away from the world, and I began to understand the urge felt by the Emperor Nicephorus II Phocas to retire to such a place, although he preferred the monastery below Mount Sinai. The visit he made to Cappadocia, together with his consort, is commemorated by the frescoes of the two of them in the Pigeon House at Çavuşin, near Zilve.

Living in such a landscape and with such antecedents, it would be surprising if the present-day inhabitants did not give a certain impression of cohesiveness. What was more surprising was their unassumed friendliness to foreign tourists, at least to us, and their lack of venality. We were constantly being offered presents of flowers and fruit and when we offered payment it was refused with genuine feelings. One small boy and girl even dismounted from their donkey and offered us a trial spin.

From the Cappadocian plateau the road eastwards descended into a wide valley backed by mountains, above which the snow-covered volcanic cone of Erciyas Daği rose 12,850 feet into the air. A big steam locomotive was racing through the valley, pulling a long train on its way to Konya and points west. Further up the valley towards Kayseri there were large vineyards, fields of sunflowers, wheat and fruit.

Kayseri, as Caesarea, was one of the cultural centres of the Roman Empire. Here there were magnificent *türbesi* (mausolea), some in forms that seem to have been inspired by nomad tents, and a Seljuk citadel of black basalt with nineteen flanking towers, built on foundations laid by Justinian in the sixth century. In the covered markets good nomad rugs were obtainable after some good-natured bargaining for less than £20. If your purse is deep enough and your inclinations lie in this direction it is only too easy to leave Anatolia looking like a door-to-door rug salesman.

It was 293 miles to Adiyaman, the setting off place for the second objective, the great tumulus of Nemrut Daği. At first we travelled through rolling country of dark earth in which the wheat was still green and women were beating wool with wooden clubs down by the abutments of bridges; then through uplands in the Tahtali Range where the streams ran away southwards to the Mediterranean, chattering over stones or else flowing silently and deeply. And we passed villages built around springs, in one of which a wedding party was enjoying itself on a roof. The only traffic we saw was lorries and Land Rovers.

There followed a long, swooping descent to Gürün, a small, pleasant place in a narrow valley under over-hanging cliffs, where we ate fried trout caught in a nearby lake and stewed lamb. While we were there a jolly party set off from the restaurant where they had gathered for another wedding, travelling in farm carts drawn by tractors.

Then into bleaker country with a few stone bothies in it and herds of shiny black horses but scarcely a human being, and up over the Hakimkhan Pass, where a river flows towards the Firat (Euphrates) and the Persian Gulf. It was burnt, brown country at this season with patches of intense green and poplars growing where the streams rise and buzzards hanging in the sky, as if suspended.

Now the road ran through a glaring wilderness of stony mountains in which the houses down by the river were equally dazzling and the sunlight and shadow played on the donkeys under the trees so that they looked like miniature zebras. The heat was truly fearful now and the tar liquid on the road. In mid-afternoon we stopped to eat delicious water melons, *karpuz*, in company with a couple of dozen drivers of monster lorries, afterwards crossing the Karahan Pass in country which reminded me of the Cheviot Hills, before descending into a plain shrouded in haze under the Malatya Mountains, where an old man was learning to drive a brand-new red tractor at a garage.

Travelling south-west, at about five o'clock we crossed the Karanlik Dere, where the wind was blowing so strongly that the river appeared to be flowing uphill. To the right was the lake of Gölbasi, with white waves on it and full of perch. Nomads were camped on its shores in their black tents. How happy they seemed to be, whatever their true condition. In Gölbasi we drank *koruk*, unfermented grape juice, at the Asfalt Palas Oteli.

We arrived at Adiyaman at sunset. There was a citadel, a mosque, notable *türbesi*, a decayed *han* to see and some undeniably picturesque shops; but we were too done in really to appreciate them. However, we had a nice dinner on a roof and a not-so-nice night in a minute hotel, the principal characteristics of which were the impossibility of escape in case of fire, a dank bathroom full of dank things and a bedroom full of bats for which there really wasn't room once we were in residence.

We rose at 3 a.m., ready to move on to Nemrut Daği; but the Manager had locked the door and was unfindable, hidden somewhere in the recesses of his maddening building. When we finally succeeded in breaking out, the driver announced that the battery of the jeep was flat. The samovar failed to deliver the goods and we breakfasted on yesterday's bread. At least we understood this kind of travel.

Eventually we got a jump start for the jeep, and once on the road things improved. The air was cold but invigorating in the open jeep, and the streets of the town had already been watered. There was a crescent moon with Venus pendant from it, and heavily wrapped men were already trotting into town, fast asleep on their donkeys.

Out in the country the shepherds had lanterns to keep their spirits up and when we stopped for a moment I could hear them groaning with fear of the night. What looked like mice scuttled across the road. First light was about 4.30 and it revealed a man praying at a crossroads.

After an hour we reached Kâhta on a tributary of the Euphrates, the ancient Nymphaios. From here a road led to Eski Kâhta, eight miles off, where mules could be hired at a reasonable price, to reach the summit of Nemrut Daği in between three and five hours.

Mist, rising from a little archipelago of islands in the river, rolled down off the range in great billows; but soon the sun rose as a ball of fire and illuminated the little villages at the foot of the mountains and the groves of holm oaks. Men and women were already in the fields threshing the grain with flails, the women wearing medieval-looking coifs and bright green, pink and yellow shifts. Savage dogs tried to commit suicide under the jeep's wheels.

The road climbed through the range by way of a gorge and eventually passed a small hotel. Later, we visited it and ate goat's cheese, olives and freshly baked flat bread in a room hung with rugs. '*There is best service in it for each tourist at Gül* [which means 'the Rose'] *Hotel/ Restaurant,*' a notice proudly proclaimed, and it was undoubtedly true.

The summit of Nemrut Daği was 6,500 feet above the sea and the air was as clear as crystal. Wild-looking Kurds with rifles guarded the site with commendable ferocity against would-be thieves and vandals, and one of the former, a tourist, was being removed as we arrived.

Here in a tent flapping in the wind, her advanced and very exposed headquarters, the distinguished, now elderly archaeologist, Theresa Goell, was already at work. She and Professor E. K. Dörner were the first to carry out a methodical investigation of the site, beginning in 1953.

Above us rose the cone-shaped tumulus more than 160 feet high and more than 480 feet in diameter, constructed for King Antiochos I Epiphanes who ruled over this, his kingdom of Commagene, in the first century BC. Under it his remains are thought to lie. Please God someone doesn't have the bright idea of removing it in order to find out, for it is built of millions, possibly billions, of smallish white stones. Now, in the early morning, against the amazingly blue sky, it looked incomparably beautiful, as if it were the true summit of the mountain, covered by a heavy night frost.

Around the base of the tumulus the King built a *hierothesion*, or temple, dedicated to his religious cult, which was part Zoroastrian, part Hellenic – he claimed descent from Darius the Persian and from Alexander the Great by virtue of a marriage alliance – and it was also to glorify his Achaemenidian ancestors, of the earliest Persian dynasty, and his kingdom of Commagene which extended from the Taurus Mountains to the Euphrates.

On the terraces and in the courtyards a series of reliefs show him greeting various Graeco/Persian deities, members of his pantheon, while inscriptions in Greek characters describe the events leading up to his accession, his reign and the nature of the religion he fostered.

High above the principal courtyards, which are to the east and west of the tumulus, he set up colossal enthroned figures of himself and of the gods in human form, guarded by statues of lions; but then, at some unknown date their heads were broken from their bodies and thrown down, whether by invaders, iconoclasts or an earthquake, has not yet been determined.

Today, these heads are set upright on the ground and, looking at them, it was easy to believe that they were the heads of stone giants buried up to their necks in the mountain, if it were not for the headless trunks on the thrones above. In the early morning the stone from which these sculptures are carved was as pale as the pebbles which composed the tumulus; but when the sun grew stronger they became warm and rosy-looking and the heads gave the impression that they were endowed with life and that blood was working in their veins.

Among them was that of Apollo/Mithra – there are various identifications and any portable literature on the subject is conflicting and inadequate – moustached and bearded, wearing a Phrygian cap and with a face covered with a network of cracks produced by the alternation of heat and cold. He is a god/man who conveyed to me, and probably no one else, for such feelings are entirely subjective, the impression that he was trying to utter what was going to be a disturbing prognostication.

A goddess of fertility wore a crown or head-dress of vines, fruit and barley, a symbol of harvest festival, while Antiochos himself, beardless, was nearer than the majority of mortals to heaven on earth. The body of his consort is buried far below on a site above the Nymphaios River.

All the heads contemplate calmly, aloofly, the tourists (who, in spite of the efforts of the Kurdish guards are – or were when I was there – breaking down the tumulus by tramping up and down its sides), and the panorama spread out like an immense relief map below their unique resting place.

That Anatolia is extensive is obvious to anyone who looks at a map of it. We really began to understand how big it was after travelling the 537 or so miles from Adiyaman to the eastward side of Lake Van by way of Malatya, Diyarbakir and Bitlis.

At Diyarbakir the road crossed the Dicle (Tigris) by a black, Roman, ten-arched bridge. Here the river flowed among plantations in which melons were cultivated, before disappearing south among bare hills. Almost everything old in this flourishing city, in a region where copper has been mined since 3000 BC, was black basalt. The black walls and towers which enclose it were built on black rock, the citadel was black and there were black mosques, black *hans* and *hamams*.

I made the circuit of the walls, nearly 3½ miles, on foot, accompanied by a host of small boys and girls, all of whom said ''Ullo' and tried to get in on all the photographs. As a result I ended up a wreck. But Diyarbakir is a good place with tented and covered markets selling ingenious artefacts: stools upholstered with strips of motor tyre, rawhide forks which collapse, like those in joke shops, if you dip them in boiling water, rush seats with children's chamber pots concealed in them, curly brass shoehorns, pack saddles, ingenious stoves made from tin as well as some of the best *ayran* I have ever tasted. In spite of the prodigious heat the ladies here wore stodgy looking bouclé or gabardine coats.

Ever eastwards with our mad driver chanting 'faaster, faaster' to himself, trying to make up for the breakdowns which became more and more frequent. He even contrived to get a puncture in the middle of an ancient hump-backed bridge over the Batman Suyu, from which it was dragged by a kindly band of soldiers condemned to spend two years on the banks of this remote river.

Now the road climbed through oak woods into what looked to me like eroded badlands, but couldn't be all that bad because good tobacco was grown. To the north were cliffs that looked like ruined casemates on the Atlantic Wall. Somewhere here we attended a lovely party under trees by a rare spring, given in honour of some men who were going to work in Germany – how strange the Ruhr must have seemed after this.

A few miles further on, at Baykan, where a new, concrete mosque was being built and the shops had trellises of branches outside to protect them from the heat, the motor car finally expired. Thankfully, we took our places in a shared taxi (*dolmus*), by far the best way of travelling in Turkey, and set off over a pass, where extensive road works were in progress, for Bitlis, hoping en route to pass through a tunnel that had been reputedly cut through the limestone by order of the Assyrian queen, Semiramis; but it had either been swept away by the road builders, or by-passed.

Bitlis is picturesquely situated in a gorge of the Bitlis River and looks like a Victorian advertisement for Turkish cigarettes, which were made here and at that time cost one Turkish lira a packet (about 3p). Once Armenian, it was appropriated by Kurdish begs in the sixteenth century, who ruled it until 1848, when it came under the rule of the Sultan –

beg is a variant of bey, a title given to senior officials in the Ottoman Empire. There was a British consulate here in the nineteenth century, and it was also the birthplace of the forebears of William Saroyan. We became very sticky here eating the good, local honey, while waiting for a bus.

The bus groaned up over a wild upland, by a road blocked with snow in winter and deposited us at Tatvan, a not very attractive watering place on the western shores of Lake Van. From here it was possible to take a car ferry and reach Van at the eastern end in eight hours; but that day was not one of the two or three a week on which it sailed, and we joined another *dolmus* in which seven of us travelled in some intimacy and arrived at Van late at night, by way of the 7,700 feet Satvan Pass. 'NOTE,' says Nagel's *Guide to Turkey*, 'Part of the Van region is closed to visitors (military zone), and it is, moreover, a very insecure area. Enquire at Ankara before setting off and, where necessary, be sure to obtain the necessary permits.' Well, we had been warned.

Seen in the early morning from the appalling, knife-edged ridge on which the citadel of Eski (Old) Van is situated, the lake – 5,600 feet above the sea – is like something in the springtime of the world. Brilliant blue, seemingly illimitable to the west – it covers 1,400 square miles. Its waters are so highly charged with mineral salts that fish can only live at the mouths of the streams which enter it, and are of a curiously soft texture, which makes swimming in them a delight. The best place for a quiet swim is Aktamar Island on which stands the beautiful Church of the Holy Cross, built by an Armenian king in the eleventh century.

The citadel of Van was one of the principal fortresses of the Urartu (Ararat) kings. The Urartians were a serious threat to the Assyrians after 800 BC and successfully resisted their attacks on Van, which they called Tuspa. They had their own script, but later adopted the Assyrian. They were famous for their bronze work, and their bronze cauldrons with handles in the form of bulls, birds and sirens have been found in Etruscan tombs in Italy, on Crete, at Delphi and at Olympia. They may be ancestors of the Etrurians. Their leaders had a passion for doing their office work underground and here, and at Toprakkale, on the mountainside above New Van, their burrowings are much in evidence.

When Urartu collapsed in the sixth century BC, the Medes occupied it, then the Persians. A typically boastful but inaccessible trilingual inscription on sheer rock begins: 'Xerxes, the Great King, King of Kings . . .' His fleet was defeated at Salamis, and his army at Plataea. Urartu was also sacked by Timur Leng in 1387.

The beginning of the end of Eski Van was in 1915 when the Armenians in the Walled City below the citadel were besieged by the Turkish army. Then it was captured and lost again by the Russians, who finally held it from March 1917 until the Armistice.

The Walled City must have been fascinating. Pre-First World War accounts describe a maze of narrow alleys and tall, huddled houses with blank, windowless façades, facing narrow streets which swarmed with Armenians and Turks and Kurds.

Now, in 1991, it looked as if it had been atomized. Nothing remained except the vestiges of the outer wall, some Seljuk mosques, the drums of minarets and some *türbesi* out on the marsh, a city occupied by goats and innumerable frogs.

New Van was not much of a place; but it did have a *hamam* and a market in which beautiful woollen stockings and rugs were made by the nomads who, at this season, pitched their tents in the plain under the Arnas Mountains, and an interesting, small museum – the best Urartian works of art were at Ankara. You could also acquire, infinitely more cheaply than at Istanbul, Armenian silver cigarette boxes decorated with repoussé work, some of which were in the form of envelopes marked *Van, 1914*, for this was where they were produced. More illicitly, for this is a region of predators, Urartian pottery, stamp seals and beautiful necklaces made from crystal, pottery beads and other stones were offered for sale.

A day's journey from Van of about 200 miles – first by way of the Lake shore, then by what was an appallingly dusty road to Agri, then eastwards towards Iran – brought one to Dogubeyazit, a frontier town known to every hippy who has taken the road to Kabul and Kathmandu. It was a sad shanty town.

Why then, you may ask, did we go to Dogubeyazit? To visit the Saray of Isak Paşa.

The Sarayi (palace) of Isak Paşa is high up in a valley behind the town, towards the Iranian frontier. A road winds up to it, past the ruins of a Kurdish village destroyed by the Turks as a reprisal for an insurrection in 1930.

Isak Paşa was one of a dynasty of feudal, Kurdish Lords. He built his palace at the end of the eighteenth century in an amazing but entirely successful *mélange* of oriental styles on a spur opposite some even more ancient buildings on the steep, eastern side of the valley – a church, later converted to a mosque, to which a minaret was also added and some fortifications built by the Genoese. It was from here that the begs controlled the cavern routes to the east and west. The view from the palace down the reddish-brown valley and across the plain to the outriders of Ararat – you can't actually see the summit – must rank as one of the wonders of the world, whether seen from the balcony of the minaret of the now unused mosque, which soars above the dome and the flagged courtyards of roofless rooms, or from the palace windows.

It is on this side that the Paşa constructed what must rank as one of the more majestically exposed water-closets – the only one that springs to mind to compete with it was the jakes 110 feet up on the outside gallery of the Longships Lighthouse off the Cornish coast, which is now no more.

When the sun sinks beyond the Sarayi the whole fantastic construction with its *hamam*, harem and audience chambers, is outlined against the sky to become an archetypal dream of an Oriental palace. For this alone the journey to the eastern extremities of Anatolia is well worthwhile.

Winter in Beijing

─────────◦⟨✕⟩◦─────────

WE CAUGHT UP with the other sixty or so members of our group at the boarding gate at Gatwick, which is already about half way to China. All of them, just as we were, excited at the prospect of their trip. What must have been the oldest, a cheerful lady in her late seventies/early eighties, had succeeded in compressing all her gear into a large envelope. As a result she never had to wait at the carousels.

There were two stops en route, the first at Zurich which had all the animation of an enormous funeral parlour; the second at Sharjah in the United Arab Emirates where there was nothing we needed except sleep.

At 1.40 a.m., London time, 14½ hours outward bound, we had our first sight of China, some 40,000 feet below through a port hole of an Air China 747.

We were over Western Kansu, a thousand miles west of Beijing, a thousand miles east of Karachi, eight time zones east of Greenwich, which made it around 9.40 a.m. local time. It would have been more time zones if China itself, by someone's brilliant legerdemain, had not been squeezed in its entirety into one gigantic time zone, all of it on Beijing time. This must make it easier for a billion Chinese to go to bed and get up in the morning at more or less the same time; and it must also be convenient for the rulers, who like to know where their loyal subjects are and what they are up to.

At least I thought we were over Western Kansu. Air China was scarcely bountiful with the information it sends back to the lumpen proletariat in tourist class, and when it does it sounds as if it has been filtered through a bowl of Air China rice, and there were no maps worth a damn in the in-flight magazine. Somewhere down below, according to my map, at around 40°N, 90°E, was the place where the Great Wall came to its western end, 2,150 miles from its beginning on a gulf of the Yellow Sea, 3,930 miles if all the branch walls and loops that have been tacked on over the ages are included.

And below us now was the Nan Shan Range, stack upon stack of knife-edge ridges. And beyond them to the north was Mongolia, with Ulan Bator somewhere in the middle of it, then nothing with a recognizable name until you got to Irkutsk on the shores of Lake Baikal in Siberia, 1,200 miles from where we were. Nice area for an unpremeditated landing!

Now we flew over some really fearful-looking country. Immense frozen uplands and dunes that looked as if they had been coated with chocolate, then given a good sprinkling of snow to freeze them all solid, the Ala Shan and the Ordos deserts; and we crossed a big bend of the Hwang Ho, the Yellow River, known as China's Sorrow because of its murderous propensities.

Then, as we turned south for Beijing we saw the Wall for the first time, silhouetted against the rising sun, which was shining through its innumerable arrow slits, roller-coasting the mountains on the borders of Shansi, with the mist rising from the valleys around it, a most wonderful spectacle.

It was strange how comparatively few people bothered to look down on China, which is only possible on the outward journey, the return being in total darkness. Could it have been that they felt that the tour didn't begin until they actually landed?

We said goodbye to the Chinese stewardesses. They had been hardworking, cheerful, kind and basically inscrutable, harbingers of all the Beijingese we were to encounter.

Our stewardess, the one who had looked after the two of us, had the face of a Bodhisattva, a being who postponed entry into nirvana in order to help others, which I suppose is as good a description of the functions of a stewardess as any.

The last time I had visited Beijing was in February 1973, when Mao was still on the throne and Chou En-lai was prime minister. I had travelled there on an Ethiopian Airways flight inaugurating a service to China from Addis Ababa. On board there had been members of the Ethiopian royal family and various ministers, many of whom were soon to be seen no more. Visitors other than diplomats were a rarity. The

Australian ambassador lent me his bike (a British BSA) to tour the city. His embassy was a makeshift one on an upper floor of what had then been the Peking Hotel, and he told me that it was so bugged that it was impossible for him to have a pee without the administration listening in.

Now, in 1992, we were droning sedately into the city on a tourist bus from the airport through what had been, nearly twenty years earlier, a plain full of decrepit single-storey villages and fields with long plastic cloches in which delicious winter vegetables were burgeoning, protected from the frost. This time the cloches were still there, but the few villages that remained were dwarfed by block after block of high-rise dwellings, like huge teeth with fillings in them. In 1973 Beijing had been a city singularly lacking in a skyline. It had been a city of horizontals. Ordinary people lived in single-storey shacks in labyrinths of lanes called *hutungs*, behind the main streets. Now the whole of the Avenue of Perpetual Peace was lined with banks, office blocks and hotels, many of them virtually skyscrapers. It looked as if it had become, with its Great Wall Sheraton, Holiday Inn Lido and Beijing International, a fortress of capitalism, and a rather boring one at that. And the process was still going on – and still is. Huge cranes traversed the sky lifting cement to the work force overhead. To make room for all this countless miles of *hutungs* had been swept away. One began to wonder whether the ancient rulers knew what was going on, hidden away in their secret places near the Forbidden City, like a lot of walnuts in boxes.

We were put up in the de luxe Beijing-Toronto Hotel – taxi drivers only knew it as the Jing Lun. Brass columns with the diameter of large trees supported, one hoped adequately, the roof of the foyer high overhead. The Western food was supportable and the Chinese restaurant excellent, patronized by locals with access to tourist money. We were given a room with a view of nothing, protested mildly and were given another with a view of the Avenue of Perpetual Peace, twice as wide as the Champs Elysées.

No sooner had we arrived than we were taken off on a lightning coach visit to the Towers of the Drum and the Bell, to the north of the Forbidden City. The towers were separated from one another by a network of alleys full of shops selling hot dumplings. That of the Bell was originally built in the reign of the Ming emperor Yong Le, about the time when the Crusades were coming to an end in the West; but it looked newer. It probably was. Everything in Beijing, including large parts of the Forbidden City, was continuously being burned down. This tower commemorated a rather foolish virgin who jumped into a vat of molten metal from which the bell was to be cast in order to improve its tone.

As the sun went down, there were fine, ochreous views of the Bei Hai Lake on which hundreds of people were skating and small children were being pulled along on sledges. By this time we were beginning to feel as if we were aspirants taking an examination for the Chinese Foreign Service in the time of the Ming: 'Travel for a minimum of nineteen hours in a closed carriage drawn by flying dragons; then set off on a cultural tour with the temperature below zero, and climb several escalades of nearly vertical steps.' We would have passed. Later we went back to the hotel and had a lovely Chinese dinner in bed.

But before passing out in room 5035, I read to Wanda an extract from the Official Travel Guide for 1992. 'Beijing has its own individuality,' its author wrote. 'Flavour of Beijing; the Quadrangle, small alley, tricycle, boiled mutton, roast duck, opera, arts and crafts – you can see, hear and feel them all only when you come to Beijing yourselves.'

'Do we have to have all this at once,' Wanda said, always ready to be helpful. 'If we do you can count me out.'

The next treat was the trip to the Great Wall and the Ming Tombs. The section of the Wall to which most visitors, however eminent, are usually taken, is at the Nankhou Pass in the Ninshan Range, where it shoots up on either side of a great gateway, at an angle of forty-five degrees in some places.

Beyond the gate there used to be very little, apart from an inn and the whole of Outer Mongolia and Siberia, to which you can still travel by train. Now there was a coach park, a 'Friendship Shop' for foreign tourists, stalls selling certificates testifying that the purchaser had climbed the Wall, and a deeply frozen dromedary, waiting for some foreign friend to be photographed astride it. There was even a cable car to the top.

Yet somehow, in spite of all this hokum, the Wall triumphed. Standing on the highest available watch tower, one of 30,000 still standing between Chinese Turkestan and the Yellow Sea, one wonders how the builders managed it, thousands of feet up in the Ninshan Range, with the streaming wind and at what cost in human life. In this section the Wall is between 20 and 30 feet high, 25 feet thick at the base, and some of the foundation stones are 14 feet long. The facing stones, the interior is rubble, are 5 feet long and 1½ feet thick.

When one of its engineers, Mêng Thien, committed suicide by order of the Emperor in 209 BC he admitted that 'in a distance of 10,000 *li* [a *li* was approximately equal to 590 yards] it is impossible that I did not cut through the veins of the earth. This is my crime.'

Thirteen Ming tombs stand at the head of what is in spring an exquisite valley among groves of trees under the Tian Shou Shan Hills, a site chosen for its supernatural as well as its aesthetic qualities. The hills sheltered the deceased from evil emanations brought from the Mongolian steppes by a wind called the *feng*. No one was allowed to live there. We weren't given any choice about which tomb to visit. We weren't taken to see the excavated tomb of Emperor Wan Li on which half a million men worked for six years, which was what we wanted to see; but to that of Yong Le, who died in 1424, an unexcavated tumulus 990 feet in diameter with a precinct of temples and pavilions entered by a great red gate. The biggest and finest palace has an amazing collection of head-dresses housed within it in a single hall more than 200 feet long with a roof supported by 32 enormous hardwood tree trunks, a room that is astonishingly cold.

Another day we took part in Beijing's answer to the marathon: the visit to the Forbidden City. For 500 years it was the most private abode for the emperors of the Ming and the Qing, together with 9,000 maids of honour and 70,000 eunuchs in the time of the Ming; the latter carried their testicles about with them in little pouches in the hope of being reunited with them in working condition when dead.

Still standing in the Forbidden City, in spite of innumerable fires, are 800 pavilions and palaces. The most fascinating and claustrophobic are the apartments of the concubines. The most famous of these, the Dowager Empress Tzu Hsi, used to dine on meals of 148 courses and took lovers from the slums, conveyed to her at night in a black, yellow-tasselled carriage. The lovers never returned to the outside world.

Of all the visitors on that particular day, said to average 10,000, only a handful were foreigners. The rest were Chinese, all busy photographing their nearest and dearest entwined round priceless, often hideous statuary, or else goggling at the dusty and badly displayed antiques, the best of which have long since been looted and removed to Taiwan.

Every morning around 7 a.m., we used to look down from our hotel room on to the Avenue of Perpetual Peace, where the temperature was around minus five degrees centigrade; during the day it rose to four or five. It had snowed the previous week and a host of female street cleaners, wearing smog masks, was trying unsuccessfully to scrape it from the pavements. They were also trying to sweep up the dust from the Gobi which gives the inhabitants and everyone else something called Peking Throat, but they only succeeded in moving it a couple of feet. You could say that they didn't have their hearts in it.

Meanwhile, an ever-moving stream of cyclists, most of them smog-masked, came pouring out of the darkness, thousands of them reinforced by pedicab drivers and men riding bikes with trailers loaded with the most amazing cargoes – half a ton of cardboard, a dozen 30ft metal rods for reinforcing concrete, an old woman transporting her grandchild in a wooden box. And there were hundreds of motor cars, some of the 80,000 official cars that our Chinese guide had told us existed in Beijing, many of which gave the impression that those they were conveying were not officials at all; taxis with mugger-proof grilles, separating the driver from the passengers, just as they do in the capitalist West, buses which started work at 5 a.m., Chinese versions of Land Rovers and the equivalent of JCBs, all roaring along the non-privileged lanes near the centre of the Avenue of Perpetual Peace (the lanes nearest the pavements in both directions were reserved for VIPs).

Almost everyone until the day warmed up a bit wore hats with ear-flaps, either sheepskin or fur. Back in 1973 these hordes, then numbering a mere five million, would have been dressed in dark blue uniforms only obtainable with ration coupons. Now they were wearing cotton or silk bomber jackets in brilliant colours lined with duck down, the best buy in Beijing at around £20 a garment. Only old men still wore clothes that were reminiscent of former times. According to *China Daily*, the official English-language newspaper, published by the regime and shoved under our door each night (we could have had the Eastern Edition of the *Wall Street Journal*, if we had been so inclined), China exported 23 million tons of down and feathers a year and 340 million US dollars' worth of down products. Twenty-three million US dollars' worth of something that floats in the air. How can they weigh it?

One of the strange things about Beijing that makes it different from a lot of other cities is that apart from a few old constructions, such as the Outer Gate of the Forbidden City on Tiananmen Square, a long stretch of genuine old palace wall on either side of it, the Beijing Hotel, and the Jesuit Observatory out to the east near the railway station, you can traverse the whole of Perpetual Peace Avenue, which is a good twelve miles long, without seeing a building that was built before the 1940s, except in the distance.

To find anything old and interesting we had to go into the *hutungs* north of Tiananmen Square, or south of it, beyond the Qian Gate, at what was, until someone knocked the walls down, the southern extremity of the Forbidden City. Here you could find areas bursting at the seams with Beijingese who had somehow avoided being shifted into the terrible high-rise blocks, many of them with non-functioning lifts.

In a not altogether successful attempt to explore these difficult-to-find places we tried every possible means of transportation. We used buses, mini-buses, taxis, the beautifully clean subway, pedicabs, known as *san lu chu* (machines with wheels), and a lot of the time we walked. One day we walked ten miles; the next, to recover, we hired a taxi for the day. It was a nice change but you don't see much from behind the grille in a taxi.

Buses were the toughest. Inside a bus it was always rush hour, whatever the time. The only thing you could possibly compare it with was being spin-dried fully clad in an enormous washing machine in the company of about a hundred other people. Hemmed in, sometimes nearly upside down, with no view of the outside world, the problem was to know where or how to get off, that is if you could get to the door in time.

Of all the ways of seeing Beijing bicycles were by far the best; but dangerous because no one in charge of any sort of vehicle – although mercifully there were no motor cycles – obeys the lights in Beijing, just as the Neapolitans firmly believe that the red is for *allegria*.

Once aboard a bicycle no one took any notice of you as a foreigner. Being on a bike was rather like donning a cloak which conferred invisibility on the wearer, but one with here and there some holes in it.

We started off at Qian Men, the gate through which the Emperor used to pass in procession, unseen by the *hoi polloi*, on his way to the wonderfully beautiful Temple of Heaven. Closed at dusk, the Qian Men opened briefly again at midnight, to allow officials to return to the Forbidden City after enjoying the pleasures of what was known as the Chinese City.

To the south was Qian Men Street, like a river in flood with humanity, its upper end filled with steamy, Dickensian-looking shops. Here, and in the east–west streets you could buy anything: bike trailers, treadle sewing machines and, in a shop besieged by customers, male and female wigs of human hair, at £13 a head. Here, in Beijing, there was not a hint of the recession that was at that time afflicting the West – a hat shop selling men's peaked caps with a bobble on top which gave the wearer a slightly mandarin-like air was packed like Harrods on sale days. On Liulichang, one of the east–west streets which sold not very real antiques (some of the *cloisonné* vases on offer were more than six feet high) the best buys were paintings on glass of Chinese courtesans, which looked as if they might have been painted around 1900 but couldn't have been. Fragile artefacts, finely framed, we bought two at £6 each, and when we came back there were already two more in the window. The shopkeeper has probably got a warehouse full of them.

In Liangshidan there was a 400-year-old shop that sold nothing but pickles, and Tongrengtang, founded in 1669, had pear juice said to be efficacious against the Peking Throat, tiger bone, snake wine and rhino horn. Conservation has yet to catch on in China. And there were shops selling felt boots, alarm clocks fitted with over-size bells loud enough to wake the dead, brass cooking pots, second-hand clothes and Chinese wind instruments. We each had an eye-test at 70p a go, but there was an eighteen-day wait for the delivery of glasses.

We had a Peking Duck dinner in a venerable restaurant. It came in various removes – smoked duck, webbed feet of duck, duck served with a sauce and eaten with pancakes, black mushrooms and an unidentifiable white root; then sesame seed cakes, duck meat sliced up, sugar balls in syrup, grapes and slices of melon which, as foreigners, cost us £10 a head.

Meanwhile, outside in the cold, men were selling hot sweet potatoes at street corners. At this end of the gastronomic price scale a delicious meal in a dumpling shop with a bottle of good beer cost between 40p and £1.20 a head. We decided to give the Hunan Restaurant a miss because its chef did with dogs what our duck restaurant did with ducks. Some places served bears' paws.

In spite of the impediments of language we were made to feel welcome as we pushed our bikes through the *hutungs* and people asked us into their houses. These were extraordinarily neat; they had to be as they were terribly crowded. Children were uncomplaining. It was rare to hear one crying. There was an almost non-existent queue to see Mao, lying embalmed in his enormous mausoleum. Officious officials drove us into his presence rather as if we were a lot of Peking ducks – hats off, wigs off, and no talking. Lying there, with only his face visible, he looked like an over-sized omelette from the McDonald's across the way at the south-west corner of Tiananmen Square.

We saw the subterranean city, level after level of it, constructed in what would have been a pretty vain hope of survival for the Beijingese if the Russians had dropped the bomb on them. All the entrances that had been open and ready in 1973 were now closed and difficult to find. We went to the opera (*pingju*). We found it hard to understand with no one to explain what was going on, but the acrobatics were astonishing.

Best of all at this time of year was life in the open air, watching the hundreds of people of all ages in parks such as the Tiantan carrying out their slow-motion callisthenics, *Taiji*, before going to work. Or mingling with the skaters on the lakes west of the Forbidden City and its frozen moats. Every day was brilliant, cold and cloudless. Most beautiful of all was the great frozen lake at the Summer Palace, with its ethereal marble bridges, like a sepia engraving in the late January sun, with no sound except the whistling of the skates on the ice; just about the only thing the Chinese didn't invent.

The Yemen

RICHARD NIXON, writing of South Yemen in 1980, called it the Cuba of the Arabian peninsula. Richard Burton, the Victorian explorer, described Aden, its principal port, as 'the coal hole of the East'. Only Freya Stark and Wilfred Thesiger seemed to have liked Yemen much in modern times, and even Thesiger said it was a tough country for walking in.

Now, in 1996, looking down on what was a pretty considerable slice of it from an airborne height of 32,000 feet, we could understand what he meant.

What we could see, all those feet below, was a terrain that looked a little bit like Marlboro Country – and was probably equally injurious to health: a lot of hot-looking sand with long, narrow mountain ranges snaking their way through it towards the Red Sea, which was all colours from the palest turquoise in the shallows to jet-black out towards the middle, where the depths exceed 7,000 feet.

It was along this coast of the Red Sea that Egyptian sailors took their ships as early as 2,500 BC in search of myrrh, a gum resin gathered from trees that grew east of Aden, in southern Yemen. The round voyage must have been more than 3,000 miles long – the Red Sea is about 1,200 miles from north to south – and would have taken anything up to two years to complete. The coast was probably as unattractive to visitors then as it is now, and later the journey was undertaken with camel caravans.

Yemen became a republic as recently as 1990, with the merging of the two, up to then mutually hostile, countries of North Yemen and South Yemen. San'a, its capital, sits on a volcanic plateau, 7,500 feet high, with mountains of up to 9,000 feet on its periphery. In the 1960s, green fields lapped the city walls, but in the last few years breaches have been made in them and the population has spilled out over the surrounding countryside, rendering it hideous with reinforced concrete and hordes of motor cycles. Only the Old City has survived, for how much longer it is impossible to say.

To penetrate its walls, as we did on a late afternoon in mid-January, is to find yourself in a world that most people from the West have long since come to believe never really existed, except in the realm of the imagination. Here, in the early evening, the sun illuminates the façades of the vast tower houses of Old San'a, five and six storeys high, flooding them with a brilliant, yellow light that bestows on them an unearthly beauty. It also illuminates those of the Old City's sixty-four minarets that are visible up the long, chasm-like streets. They look like space vehicles about to take off for some celestial, Islamic destination. But San'a is older than Islam and if, as some Yemenis say, it was founded by Shem, the son of Noah, then it is very old indeed.

These houses are constructed at various levels from black basalt, tufa and sun-baked brown and bright new-fangled bricks, some of them set in alternating geometric patterns, the window frames whitewashed. One of the most difficult tasks a writer can set him or herself is to describe the architecture of such a house, and I confess I'm beaten. The windows were made from slices of alabaster, now being replaced by stained glass framed in brilliant white gypsum. Originally these houses were built to accommodate several interrelated families, and each lofty room had a specific use. There was a well and separate lavatories on every floor. On the top floor was the *manzar* with the best views. The next below it was the *mafraj*, where the menfolk gathered, as they still do, to chew *qat*, the universal male panacea. The interiors of these houses were white-washed from top to bottom.

The interior staircases of a tower house lead up and around a central pillar known as 'The Mother of the House', and if this pillar was ever to show signs of stress, then, according to custom, the house might have to be completely rebuilt around a new pillar.

One or two of these great houses offered simple accommodation for the more fragile sort of traveller, and we stayed in one – the Golden Daar. It had a nice, shaded garden and the weather was still warm enough to eat outside. Having left our locked-up baggage and inspected our room, which was so high up that we practically needed oxygen to survive in it, and having very nearly trepanned ourselves on one of the picturesque low stone lintels, which are only a few feet high, and suitable only for the passage of dwarves, we set off for the Salt Souk, otherwise known as the Suq al-Milh. This souk, the biggest in San'a, comprises forty smaller souks, all of which are guarded at night by men who look down on them from watchtowers.

The souk is reached by cavernous streets deep in errant plastic bags, some of which look as if they might conceivably date back far enough to be original prototypes of this particular artefact. No plastic bag emerges from the Suq al-Milh once it escapes from human hands. It simply goes on whirling around its streets for all eternity.

It was on the way to the souk that we were joined by our first welcoming committee, composed of six or seven beautiful, dark-eyed children. The oldest was about ten, the youngest looked as if she had only just relinquished the breast as a source of sustenance. All except the smallest one had gleaming white teeth of the sort you see in Colgate ads. All were more than anxious to make our acquaintance, and the air rang with cries of 'Allo! Allo!', 'Where are you coming from?' and 'What's your name?' To which we replied appropriately, having our Lonely Planet Arabic phrase book conveniently to hand, which left them in stitches.

Whenever and wherever we reached a fresh destination on our travels through Yemen in the succeeding days, we found a similar reception committee awaiting us. None of their members ever asked for money. All of them asked for pens. Take a few dozen Biros to Yemen and help the literacy rate to rise. Their own toys were of the simplest description. The most popular one, used by boys, was a wheel with a wire handle, which they pushed in front of them in a state of semi-euphoria, pretending to be driving a car; others played mysterious games involving what looked like cabbalistic signs scratched on the cobblestones. Some had marbles, but not many. One had what he described as a *futbol*. It was the children of whom we had our most vivid memories in Yemen.

Down in the souk and everywhere else in mountainous Yemen in the afternoon, all the men looked as if they were suffering from a severe attack of the gumboils, or something worse, with one cheek – always the same one – swollen up. These were the chewers of *qat*. a mild narcotic said to have a similar effect to a moderate dose of amphetamine, contained in the leaves of the *qat* plant, *Catha edulis*, which needs only water to make it sprout. The lump on the cheek is where the chewer conceals the residual goo, and is not permanent. The bigger the lump the more highly you are regarded by your fellow *qat* chewers.

Qat is not supposed to be a dangerous drug, and specifically the only ill effect it appears to have is on the take-home pay of the users, which is considerably reduced. Wives hate it because having a husband on *qat* is a great strain on the domestic economy. It isn't a drug people are secretive about, most people chew it at parties, of which the President's are the most prestigious.

We entered the souk through an archway and our infant bodyguard melted away, leaving us to the grown-up Yemenis in what is still one of the largest medinas (walled open spaces) in the Islamic world. Most of the women were wearing the *sharshaf*, the black skirt, black cape, black head-covering and veil introduced into San'a by Turkish women only half a century ago. Some wore the *abaya*, a loose black cloak peculiar to San'a. Some wore brilliant garments known as *sitaras*, over baggy trousers; these were women from the mountains and from the Tihama, the coastal plain on the shores of the Red Sea. Most were veiled, hiding all but their huge almond eyes, the edges of the lids blackened with antimony, which are left uncovered to dazzle the beholder and, if the beholder is a male, probably to disturb him, too. The women's hands were decorated with extravagant curlicues made with henna. The women were outnumbered by the men, as they are all over Yemen. The men mostly wore the *futah*, a sort of skirt that ends below the knees and is supported by a belt and worn with a shirt and Western-style jacket. It is not as bad as it sounds. In the belt those of any consequence, or aspiring to be, wear the *djambia*, a ceremonial dagger with a hilt at its most luxe made of ivory or the last of the rhino horns, which cost a fortune. The Yemenis are principally responsible for the near-disappearance of the rhinoceros from the face of the earth. Most of the younger men wore the chequered red and white head-dress, made in Korea and Japan for export to the Arab world.

By now it was growing dark and the lights were coming on in the cavern-like shops and serpentine streets. Last to close were those in the spice bazaar, where you could smell a lot of the goods without actually seeing them: sacks of cardamom, lentils, coffee husks (roasted to make

Cycling along the arcadian Canal de L'Ourcq.

The Canal de L'Ourcq: 'Eventually its towpath took us under the autoroutes west of Paris at Pont de Bundy, which is decorated with inspired graffiti.'

Previous page Two degrees west – knocked out on the edge of the Cheviot Hills, first day.

Opposite The coast of southern Turkey.

Above A shepherd (left) in Pamukkale, Anatolia, wearing one of the huge felt cloaks rather like sentry boxes which are known as *kepenek*.

Left The *peri bacalari*, or fairy chimneys of Anatolia 'which resemble gigantic phalli or fungi, according to one's state of mind . . .'

Me in Tiananmen Square: in Beijing 'being on a bike was rather like donning a cloak which conferred invisibility to the wearer . . .'

Above The multi-storey palace
of the Imam Yahya, built in
the 1930s, Yemen.

Left The Salt Souk, also
known as the Suq al-Milh,
Yemen.

St Aldhelm's Head seen from Swyre Head.

The Roman Catholic chapel in the grounds of Lulworth Castle, designed to resemble a pagan temple. This was the first Roman Catholic church to be built in England since the Reformation.

West Bucknowle, our Dorset house.

less strong coffee), cloves, sultanas, dried apricots and cherries, cinna-
mon and so on.

When it was quite dark, from the greatest of San'a's great mosques,
al-Jami'al-Kabir, came the muezzin's call to the evening prayer. It was
the most powerful call that I have ever heard in the Islamic world
and caused all the calls emanating from other mosques to pale into
insignificance. That night we ate in one of the restaurants on the road
that encircles the city. Evenings tended to be rather long and not *très
gai*; nobody told us that as a visitor you were allowed to bring a litre
of booze with you, so we had none. (You should also bring plenty of
literature, a couple of 100-watt light bulbs, a tennis ball cut in half to
use as a bath plug, and candles and matches. Most important, bring a
member of the other sex who doesn't snore.)

In the company of our companion, driver and guide, we quartered
the wild and mountainous country to the north and east of San'a, as
far as the shores of the Red Sea. He was about forty, and had seven
children aged between four and twelve, whom we subsequently met. He
was a prodigious smoker – sixty a day – and a great chewer of *qat*.
From time to time he sang Yemeni songs and went through a stack of
cassettes. His wife was very orthodox, and he was a strong supporter of
the veil. All his children knew exactly what they were going to be, apart
from the four-year-old, who presumably wanted to be an engine driver.
They were going to be lawyers, bankers, secretaries, soldiers, that sort
of thing. Who was going to sweep the streets in a few years' time when
they had majored in such subjects? Fortunately for them there is a body
of people know as *Akhdam* whose job it is to perform such menial
tasks.

At Rayda, just north of San'a, there was a large and extremely animated market that took place at the foot of the crumbling mud walls of
what had been an imam's palace. The roads leading to it were planted
with eucalyptus trees and wattle, and along the route there were remains
of motor vehicles that looked as if they had been gnawed by giant rats.
Here, along the walls, men were dusting potatoes with brooms – it was
a pretty dusty market – and goats were selling at £12 a head, the smallest
being tended by girls of about six. The air was alive with the complaints
of sheep, and there were hordes of heavily veiled women selling chickens
that looked as if they would have been happier dead. Overlooking this

astonishing place there was a huge minaret. Here, as everywhere else we went, every man had a rifle and the favourite was a Kalashnikov.

Out in the country we drove up the Wadi Dhahr, a deep green trench flanked by red, eroded mountains. Vines were growing on trellises behind mud and sandstone walls, and in the fields there was alfalfa, and garlic, peppers, onions, tomatoes, peaches and coriander.

Looming over all this, appearing to sprout from a high rock, was the multi-storey palace of the Imam Yahya, built in the 1930s, with a solitary cypress growing near it and what looked to me like a banyan tree. High above the wadi, terraced fields with retaining walls built of basalt followed the contours of the mountains. Brown at this time of year, they would soon be green when the monsoon rains arrived. And on all the peaks and ridges there were watch towers. After this, on to Shibam, at the foot of an immense cliff with the remote village of Kawkaban on top of it that looked as if it was about to crash down on Shibam, 1,000 feet below.

We ate lunch at Shibam, in a long, lofty room with bright carpets – blue, yellow, red – on the floor. Plants in pots, a sort of heather. A silver-hilted sword in a silver scabbard on the wall. Gypsum window frames and stained glass. The only sounds the droning of the wind and children playing in the street. The meal was served by a young veiled woman: freshly baked bread soaked in yoghurt with a hot sauce of tomatoes and green peppers, followed by rice with saffron and cooked vegetables – potatoes, okra, tomatoes, garlic, onions, coriander and spices. Then chicken, or lamb with lentils, beans, chickpeas, eggs, fenugreek, coriander and chillies. Then fried eggs with tomatoes and onions. Then *bint al sahn* ('daughter of the clerk'), a sort of cake eaten with clarified butter and honey, and finally tea with cardamom and sugar: in all 800 riyals (about £4) for three.

After all this, to Kawkaban by way of Wadi Nahim. Fuelled with *bint al sahn* we could probably have floated up there. The road, only completed in 1994, wound up past white-flowering almond trees, and past a lonely graveyard, into a wilderness of stone. Away to the west was a huge rock with what looked like the Ark on top of it.

To Amrann, a windy town with litter swirling through the streets, many wonderful mud houses and a market abandoned by the Jews who left Yemen for Israel (although there are still a few in the north of the country). Their shops, now closed for ever, had roofs supported by stone columns.

In the market we bought a beautiful marine fossil for 100 riyals and were subsequently offered an almost identical one on a mountainside outside the town for 50.

Now we climbed over a mountain range on a road built by the Chinese, who had erected a sort of mini-pagoda at the foot of the pass. (If not built by the Chinese, roads in Yemen are built by Russians or Germans.) The mountains here looked like old bones and black clouds were steaming over them. We ate at a place called Khulan Affar, in what looked like a lock-up garage, more than 9,400 feet up on the mountainside. It was the same sort of food as the previous day at Shibam – less copious, but with more of the delicious bread.

The clientele were heavily armed but friendly – we hoped – tribesmen, who arrived in their Toyotas and from whom, apparently, we could have purchased a gift-box of hand grenades if we had been so inclined. This place had a dangerous feeling about it.

The next step on the way to the Red Sea was Az-Zaydiya, where the people live in bee-hive huts with roofs made of sorghum, wear tall straw hats, in which they keep their lunch, and have an African appearance. Down here it was very warm after the chill of the mountains, and there were elephant trees – small and mushroom-shaped, with pale trunks. And there were camels, their shapes often distorted by the mirage, with timid white birds perching on their backs. Some of the less fortunate were blindfolded and forced to walk in endless circles, crushing sesame seeds between stones. Great piles of sorghum and sacks of henna were being sold by the roadside, and off the road there was a market where thousands of men – no women – were trading goats in the shade of crumbling walls.

The hideous wind and dust-swept port of Al-Hudaydah was our introduction to the Yemeni shores of the Red Sea. Here you could buy a baby shark or a Chinese motor tyre from the Woosung Company, as the spirit moved you. We settled for lunch – fish split in two and grilled with herbs, served with a wonderful but unidentifiable sauce.

We spent the next night at Al Mahwit, a small town in the mountains. That evening three members of a French group who were staying in the same hotel as us were stabbed in the street by a man described by the police as a lunatic. Soon after we returned to Dorset we heard that another French group, fourteen of them in all, had been taken hostage by some tribal group, but subsequently released.

This was in 1996, two years before the shooting of hostages in December 1998.

A Brief Trip to
the Pontine Archipelago

WE WERE on our way to Anzio, in June 1997, from where we were going to take the hydrofoil to Ponza. The entire length of the road from Rome, only forty kilometres to the north, was heavily developed. If we are to believe Charles Dickens, down there on a visit in 1846, even then it was pretty ghastly. 'An undulating flat,' he wrote, 'where few people can live; and where for miles and miles there is nothing to relieve the terrible monotony and gloom.' It is not surprising that it was gloomy, being a highly malarial area until Mussolini appeared on the scene and reclaimed much of the marshland. But then Dickens, to my mind, was a rather condescending traveller, anyway. He didn't much like Rome, either. He thought it looked like London, which is a bit much.

At Anzio, we got our driver to take us to the British War Cemetery on the outskirts of the town, with its 1,056 headstones of those who died there in the landings in 1944, and subsequently. As are all British war cemeteries, even the most remote, this one is beautifully looked after – the grass a brilliant green in contrast with the already burnt-up foliage outside its walls, the beds alive with geraniums, daisies and pansies. The young gardener, Mario Moretti, who looks after the cemetery, is so blackened by the sun that where he sits in the shade in his dark clothes only his eyes are visible. He has planted hedges with an evergreen shrub which in season bears a yellow flower that is sweet-smelling. He loves his cemetery and its occupants.

The other cemetery, a splendid one and much larger, is the US cemetery at Nettuno, next door to Anzio. Here are the graves of 7,862 servicemen who died in the fighting on the way from Sicily to Rome; a further 3,094 went missing and were never identified.

To Anzio at last, its principal piazza resembling a cooking pot on the boil. Here, a tall semi-circle of white and muffin-coloured houses looked down on the port. And on the seaward side, beyond the mole, there was a small, sandy beach, not all that much of a sandy beach for people like ourselves who had flown all this way to get to it; but small children were paddling around on it, and digging themselves in and they seemed to find it all right. Offshore there wasn't an island, Ponzan or otherwise, to be seen let alone an archipelago which is what we were bound for.

There was a restaurant. It was cool and nice, with white curtains. It had blue and white tablecloths, which matched the blue and white umbrellas on the beach below. The walls were white with a fishy-blue frieze high up on them. The waiters looked competent. This was a serious eating place. Four undoubtedly serious middle-aged men, who looked like *procuratori* (lawyers) with whom you would not wish to tangle and with whom you would need a long spoon to sup, were eating away silently, with their napkins tucked into their shirts.

After some deliberation we ordered, having no difficulty in rejecting the *aragosta* (lobster) at 80,000 lire (£30) a plate. We settled for *gnocchi di patate* with shell fish and pecorino cheese and then *fritto misto di mare*, with a salad of rocket and tomatoes and some good local white wine, for 30,000 lire each.

We then went out along the mole to see fish being off-loaded from one of the late-arriving boats. This particular one had had a pretty poor catch: some red mullet and conger eels and a few swordfish. The fisherman whose property they were attempted to sell one of the larger ones to me. But neither Wanda nor I were keen on swordfish. They are usually too dry when grilled, although there are other, juicier ways of preparing them.

'Have you any use for a large, morning-gathered swordfish?' I asked Wanda, having told the fisherman that I had nothing to cook it in. It was meant as a joke but she doesn't always understand when I am joking.

'Why do you always want to buy tings you don't need?' she said, meanly, being the biggest collector of arcane objects the world has ever seen.

We set off for Ponza at 3.15 p.m. from the *Molo Innocenziano*, travelling in an *aliscafo* (hydrofoil) that was only half full. Although the Italian school holidays had not yet started, there were a number of schoolboys on board. They had all presumably escaped from the same institution, as they were all wearing the same colour long-peaked caps which someone invented for US presidents to play golf in. After a bit they got bored with zooming about and gazed abstractedly at their reflections in the windows, while picking away at their hooters. The only place you could get any air in this *aliscafo* was on a short stretch of midships deck, open to the sky. It was sad weather now. The sun had gone in. The sea was like olive oil.

After an hour or so the first islands of the Ponza group began to raise themselves out of the sea: to starboard, two high, cone-like peaks, part of a complex of rocks and stacks off the island of Palmarola; and to port, what looked like a rather badly sliced piece of Cheddar turned out to be the island of Zannone. Both of them were uninhabited. Then we went through a sort of sound between Ponza and Isola di Gavi, both covered with scrub, and some cliff-hanging, box-like houses in various pastel shades.

Then, suddenly, the sun came out and everything was bathed in a brilliant, ochreous light. We were in a large bay and on its shores there were more of the box-like houses, more than the eye could cope with. They were on every hillside, and in every intervening valley, down which they appeared to be cascading seawards.

And when we finally came into the port of Ponza, which was crammed with vessels of all shapes and sizes, and the *aliscafo* was tied up alongside the mole where the port officials had their offices, we were confronted by a waterfront more wonderful than any we had so far seen elsewhere in the Mediterranean – part of a never-never land that might have been designed by Rex Whistler and Ronald Firbank.

High above the water were the administrative offices of what had been, in the eighteenth century, the Bourbon Governor, and were now the seat of the *commune*. In 1779, the Bourbons of Naples invested heavily in the islands to guarantee the security of the colonists from the mainland, whom they had encouraged to settle there.

Painted a brilliant lemon-yellow, the Governor's old offices looked down on Piazza Carlo Pisacane. Pisacane was a well-known revolutionary, a thorn in the backsides of the Bourbons. He hijacked a large ship on its way from Genoa to Sardinia and then proceeded to shoot up Ponza, at the same time releasing from the goal a number of prisoners, some of whom were genuine dangerous criminals, not, as he imagined, political prisoners at all.

And down on the water's edge, on the south side of the harbour, built on a gentle curve that would end up in a semi-circle if only it could be extended far enough, were the *abitazioni* of the Ponzans, the lowest buildings, almost at sea level, painted externally in what is known as *sangue di bue*, ox-blood, mostly store rooms for fishermen's gear with white-framed doorways leading to dark, mysterious interiors. And above them, overlooking Via Pisacane, enfilades of elegant, mostly white-washed houses, which were fed with water from reservoirs.

Behind the Governor's offices, which backed on to the barracks, was the fine, domed church of SS Trinità e dei Santi Silverio e Domitilla (Silverio being the patron saint of Ponza). And high above everything else, the Great Tower, built by Alfonso of Aragon between 1479 and 1481 on the foundations of the Roman Villa of the Emperor Augustus, which was heavily damaged when it was bombarded by two British frigates in 1813, and was used by the Fascists as a prison, now a hotel.

Apart from the Great Tower, building in Ponza – in what was to be an unusually beautiful and practical experiment in urbanization – was entrusted by the Bourbon King of Naples to two men: Antonio Winspeare, an English major of Engineers in the Bourbon army, and Francesco Carpi, a Neapolitan architect. Together they rebuilt the port on the foundations of the original Roman construction.

We were met on the mole, near the site of what had been the very modest Governor's Palace, by Carlo Marcone, who was a *geometria*, a surveyor, and was also the head of the *Pro-Loco* – the local tourist office.

He was a very tall young man who knew everybody and was not only omniscient but omnipresent. He never told us where to meet him but literally popped up wherever we happened to be, except on one occasion when he said he was going to pop up in Piazza Pisacane at a certain time and never popped up at all.

He took us to our hotel in his car. Ponza is only 7.5 km long and 2.3 km wide, tapering at one point to a stretch so narrow (200 metres) that you have to be careful not to fall into the Tyrrhenian Sea.

With only three roads of any consequence on the entire island, you might think that hardly any of the Ponzans would find it worthwhile to have a car; but they do. In what is presumably a race to keep up with their fellow islanders socially, they have got themselves into a situation in which there is said to be a car for each one of its 3,000 inhabitants. And, madly, visitors, who arrive in July in enormous numbers from Rome and Naples, are allowed to bring their vehicles, too.

It is impossible to find any accommodation in the entire Ponzan archipelago in the summer, unless, like Eton, you have been put down for it at birth. To get to the hotel Carlo took us through a labyrinth of lanes, lined with freshly whitewashed, almost identical, flat-roofed houses, some with strange owl-like chimneys. At this hour all the streets were deserted. This was the time when the inhabitants get their heads down. The owner of the hotel was a widow. The hotel itself was clean and decent. The hall was adorned with large sea shells, a Roman anchor and Roman amphorae – well, they looked Roman – fished from wrecks in the Tyrrhenian Sea.

The Signora, keen to impose half-pension on us for what was still the low season, something we had been anxious to avoid unless she was a first-class cook, asked us what we would like for dinner. We ordered spaghetti *con vongole*, roast chicken and white wine – it is almost impossible to find red wine in these islands. We ate our not very good dinner on a terrace overlooking a large excavation in the soft, volcanic tufa, a meal suddenly interrupted by a discharge of mortar bombs in honour of San Silverio, which exploded with shattering reports and continued to do so every evening at the same hour until the passing of his saint's day.

At last, having been nineteen hours outward bound from Heathrow, we retired, whacked, to a pleasant and lofty bedroom with a balcony. The wind, which had got up, was pleating the white muslin curtains and howling like a banshee in a nearby chimney. The next morning we were woken at 7 a.m. by what sounded like a thousand *motorini*, but was only really about ten, as they roared down the narrow alleys of the Port, driven by their presumably stone-deaf, lunatic owners. Once at sea level they continued to drive everyone mad for the rest of the day before roaring back up the hill to have it off with their wives and eat gigantic pastas.

On our more sedate passage down to the Port on foot we met a widow in deepest black who had just baked some bread and had had it blessed by the priest in the church of San Silverio. The real business of Ponza, social, political and almost every other activity, including screwing the visitors in due season, takes place outside under the clock tower on the terrace of the Piazza Carlo Pisacane. And there are few greater pleasures, in terms of doing absolutely nothing, than sitting out on this terrace under the ilex trees in front of the cafés, with the evening sun shimmering on the leaves, and watching the Ponzans and the visitors from Rome and Naples performing the *passeggiata* along Via Pisacane, following the arc of Winspeare's and Carpi's masterpiece. Meanwhile, outside the church of SS Trinità, boys were playing basket ball, so tall some of them that in their white gear they looked as if they had been extruded from a giant toothpaste tube.

Before we set off in a boat for a *giro* of the island, I had a rapid early morning haircut, rapid because I haven't got much to cut. From the barber's chair I could see the harbour, which was already pulsating with activity. We set off at 10.30 in what we hoped was the good ship SS *Redentore da Benedetto*, bright yellow with an orange band round it.

On board were two priests. One of them, an Australian of about forty-five, was wearing an un-priestly yellow swimming costume and was a great exponent of the crawl. The other one, older, with a hairy body, was something, he let us know, rather big in the Vatican, but living outside it, which sounded ideal. The two of them photographed each other, displaying banks of expensively capped teeth. Altogether we were fourteen passengers, including two married couples and some very comely Italian girls.

The weather was hot and cloudless. As we departed we passed a little domed, silver lighthouse on the mole near the Governor's residence. What followed was a recital of colours: fragile-looking tufa cliffs, brilliant red and white rocks, Bourbon forts, vineyards producing sweet wine. A huge, Cambridge-blue stack with maquis growing on top of it, supported on prongs, like a huge, rotten tooth, a bit like the one in Calabria, with the sea flowing through it. Others, also light blue, looked like castles melting in the heat.

The beaches were shingle and scree, the water deep blue indigo, the most wonderful we have ever been in when we were finally allowed over the side, like swimming in champagne.

In the narrow passage between Ponza and the outlying island of Gavi pale green water heaved over a wicked-looking reef and two men fished close to it from a small boat. At Cala Felice huge boulders balanced one on top of the other, and a great stack looked like the *Titanic* going down. At Cala Fonte there was a minute harbour in the tufa with room for half a dozen small boats, and *ginestra* (broom) was growing close by the water. We crossed the channel from Faraglioni to the south-western cliffs of Cala Brigantina, a huge complex of stacks and cliffs some of them more than 160 feet high, sheer to the sea.

We had a delicious lunch of pasta and wine moored near to stacks which must be some of the wonders of the world. It had been a memorable day. We returned in the evening to dine on pasta and more *vongole* at the Ristorante Capriccio. Here in Ponza we were in serious danger of being vongoled to death.

The next day we met an inhabitant of Ponza on the street where the Governor's Palace was situated and asked him what the trees with whitewashed trunks were. '*Sono piante per pazzi*,' he replied, plants for madmen. In fact they were holm oaks. A little mad ourselves, we then climbed in terrible heat to the cemetery at Punta della Madonna. Here the tombs were as big as a bijou house, and you could look down on the extraordinary diversity of colours in this volcanic but dormant island.

That Sunday morning Ponza was awash with people but then, in the afternoon, they gradually drifted away back to the mainland. We saw a priest blessing a new inflatable lifeboat for the Carabinieri on the Molo, in the presence of the Capitano del Porto and the town band. Drinks were served at little tables, although sampled only gingerly, and the mortar bombs exploded again overhead with their terrible bangs. But by now we were used to noises. Every morning began with the roar of the *motorini* and someone apparently tunnelling under our room. We would then recover over a breakfast of croissants and packets of that sort of jam that is always stickier than real jam.

We visited the Ghiaia Beach, by way of a Roman tunnel through the tufa which was partially blocked by debris. We then took a bus to the village of La Forna, all white, with a church and not a soul in sight. Then down to a stony beach by endless steps where the tufa was red hot.

We took a boat from the Porto to Spiaggia di Frontone, below the Bourbon fort, the Fortino di Frontone. Here, the beach was sand below high water, shingle above it. Along its length was a single line of beach beds and umbrellas. At one end a large cave opened out under grey cliffs. The weather was siroccoish. Altogether there were no more than about seventy people on it, mostly Italian, and only a few young children.

There were two small restaurants at opposite ends of the Spiaggia. The one at the northern end was nicer, the *padrone* more biddable. It had plantations of prickly pears, hibiscus and red bougainvillaea, and white and pink oleanders, and a cane roof supported on whitewashed columns; and some trees, a sort of acacia with ivy growing up them. Two girls at the next table were playing cards with a black boy of about ten who was wearing orange shorts. We ordered lunch from a wooden gazebo where the proprietor was standing – *panini* with salami and mortadella and German draught beer. The furnishings were bright blue, and the sound of the sea in the background as it crawled up and retreated down the beach completed the ambience of a place where it was pleasant to linger.

The Saint's Day finally arrived. Bunting whipped in a strong breeze around the lemon and white church. The town band played 'O Sole Mio', 'Ciaou, Ciaou, Bambina' and the 'Canzo del Santo-Anima Mia'. The Bishop and the priest were wearing expensive cassocks, and everyone had made an effort to look their best. The visitors to Ponza, who had come all the way from New York to look up their relatives, were the envy of all the island women on account of their splendid handbags. Eventually the Saint appeared through the open door of the church amidst the deafening explosions of the mortar bombs. He rested on a bed of gladioli and red carnations and these carnations were thrown down on the heads of the faithful. We scrimmaged for possession of them as, they are of good augury. San Silverio was then zoomed off along Via Pisacane to begin his inspection of the fleet assembled in the port. The celebrations were brought to an end with a grand fireworks display at midnight.

Below the Purbeck Hills

FOR ALMOST TWENTY YEARS from 1977 to 1996, we lived in an old house perched on a hill close to the Purbeck Hills. When we first saw it – we had been recommended to have a look at it by a friend – we knew immediately that this was the house we had to have, whatever its condition.

The house was the property of the widow of a retired regular army colonel. She was a nice old lady with a penchant for lighting bonfires all over the grounds of what was a quite extensive property.

The only materials she used to ensure combustion were the usual ones – damp, dead leaves of which there were tons all over the place in autumn, twigs which came sailing down from high overhead, jettisoned by a colony of rooks who had borne them aloft only to find that they were sub-standard for their nest-building operations, or had simply dropped them by mistake. When all her fires, a dozen or so, were on the go at any one time, the place looked as if it was being subjected to a gas attack, or rather like a Red Indian encampment might look during an exchange of smoke signals.

She also made prodigious quantities of jam which she put on sale down by the lodge at the main gate, with a tin can to act as a cash box for the customers to put the money in, which not all of them remembered to do. We did the same with daffodils of which there were enormous numbers.

And in the New Year she used to invite little bands of ladies to pick the snowdrops which made such a welcome show in the surrounding woods, with which they used to decorate the wards in the local cottage hospital, in Swanage.

When we finally took possession of the house in the depths of a freezing winter we let it be known that this band, or similar bands of ladies, would be welcome to pick as many snowdrops as they liked, but over the years the numbers of ladies steadily decreased until one early new year there were a lot of snowdrops but no ladies to pick them.

She was also a bit forgetful, and every time we met over the succeeding weeks and months, and we met pretty frequently, it was necessary to reintroduce ourselves at some length, and also to explain what was the purpose of our visit, as if we had never met before.

It was selling her beloved house that we both felt finally killed her (she died in a nursing home soon after leaving it).

The house was called West Bucknowle – a Saxon name signifying Bucca's Noll. The next large house to the east of ours was Bucknowle House; it was late Victorian, built, as ours was, on the foundations of an early edifice, possibly older than ours.

Our house probably dated from sometime between 1790 and 1840. Building patterns for such a house – which was very much like a West Country rectory – were rare in Purbeck, though common in north and west Dorset, and were slow to change.

No one could tell us much about our house. The Dorset County Council in Dorchester were unforthcoming, not because they were secretive but simply because they didn't know anything. All they did, in answer to our inquiries, was send a lady from Dorchester to slap a Grade II Preservation Order on it. She didn't know anything about it, either. Even the vast, compendious *Inventory of Historical Monuments in the County of Dorset*,* which lists and describes quite small cottages in Church Knowle, our neighbouring village, had nothing on West Bucknowle House, or Bucknowle House, apart from mentioning Bucknowle as being a 'settlement' mentioned in Domesday.

The house was built of stone, faced with stucco and painted the colour of muffins. It was two storeys high and had large gutters which attracted huge quantities of smelly, decaying leaves, and these gutters had to be cleaned out twice a year – a job which I found difficult, balanced on a long wooden ladder, with Wanda keeping her foot on the bottom rung, twenty feet below.

When we bought it, the house was in a pretty rough state. One day,

---

* Published by the Royal Commission on Historical Monuments, 1970.

while we were camping on the premises in order to keep the builders up to scratch, which they tended not to be if left by themselves, I dropped my toothbrush in an upstairs bathroom, and eventually found it in the dining room down below.

But none of this really mattered. The important thing was that, since it was built, the house had never been mucked about with. The rooms were perfectly proportioned, neither too high, nor too low, and there were some really beautiful fireplaces, one of which we brought from our previous house in Devon. The kitchen on the ground floor was fitted with a cast-iron Herald range that was still listed in the Army and Navy Stores catalogue of 1937–8. And there was an enormous cellar, the same shape as the house itself, which kept white wine at the right temperature without recourse to refrigeration. The bathroom that had taken my toothbrush away had a white-enamelled terracotta bath in it, encased in mahogany. It was so deep that no one ever contrived to fill it completely.

The first sight of the house was from the place where the pillar box still stands, by the lodge on the Corfe Castle/Church Knowle road. From there you could see it, high on its hill, partly hidden by enfilades of horse chestnuts and enormous dying beeches that were still in the same state of dissolution as they were when we left the place, years later. And there was an orchard below it, which gave the magical impression that the house itself was sprouting up out of the trees. In this orchard we set up an obelisk which was twenty feet high and weighed more than twenty tons.

Hidden away among the chestnut trees, there was a gigantic oak whose branches had grown around a nursery fireguard. Some Regency children had probably used it to make a tree house, and had then forgotten about it. It finally fell from the tree around 1994.

There were three great views from the house: a distant view of what are the truly colossal ruins of Corfe Castle, away to the east; a long vista, looking north from the front porch across the valley, to the Pur-beck Hills, which seemed to loom above the road like a tidal wave about to break; but the best view was from the south side, the back of the house, down a long tunnel of beech trees as far as Kingston village with its great church of St James, built for the 3rd Earl of Eldon by George Edmund Street, the architect of the Law Courts in London, a work which took six years and was completed in 1880, his masterpiece. An Arcadian vista.

There was a kitchen garden with raspberries (summer and autumn varieties), asparagus – not very successful – blackcurrants, redcurrants and mange-tout. And there was a deep, freshwater well – well, fairly fresh – and a little slate-roofed stone building that had once housed a privy which some people remembered ladies repairing to when there were garden parties. The back garden was so sheltered from the wind, or most winds, that you could light a match while a force 9 gale was raging overhead.

And there was wildlife in such superabundance that on several occasions when it began to get us down we used to think about selling up and going away.

There were rabbits, but they were not really much of a menace, and grey squirrels; and there were badgers. The badgers had excavated several truly enormous setts that looked like miniature tumuli, that is if you could see them, as they were overgrown with thorns and were hidden in the most impenetrable parts of our woods.

In the last years before we sold the house the badgers launched what seemed to be ever more violent attacks on our back lawn in search of grubs. They started methodically at the far, southern end of it. We tried everything to move them on. We even left out plates loaded with delicacies such as slugs and worms that we thought might take them away from their beloved grubs, but they just polished these off and then moved on to the grubs, the main course. All of this without so much as a thank-you.

The moles even put me off *The Wind in the Willows*, something I wouldn't have believed possible previously. Sometimes when the worms they lived on were close to the surface after rain, you could see the lawn heaving like a green sea. To walk on it after a mole attack was like going for a walk on the Goodwin Sands. We tried everything. We put bottles upside down over the entrances to their mole holes, hoping that the low moaning note made by the wind in them would drive them away, but it didn't. Presumably they were tone deaf. We tried mole traps which were supposed to nip the mole's nose as it zoomed along one of its innumerable passages. This way we caught about half a dozen, but I gave up when I sprang the trap on my finger. You had to wear gloves when setting these traps because moles don't like the smell of human hands. The most ridiculous thing I ever did, mole-wise, was to attach a length of rubber pipe to the exhaust of a Volkswagen van, then put the other end down a mole hole. As the pipe wasn't a very good fit, I had to hold it on to the exhaust and I soon began to doze off, poisoning myself with carbon monoxide. Had I not come to, it would have looked like a mole-inspired suicide. Eventually we found that the most effective way of shifting moles was to shove rags steeped in creosote down their holes.

Meanwhile on the surface of our little kingdom, near to if not by the sea, once the young rose shoots, of which there were large numbers, were out on the bushes, so were the deer of every sort out in force to snip them before our eyes. They snipped and ate them as delicately and appreciatively as a gourmet might a helping of Malossol caviar.

They were real problems, the deer. On Bucca's Noll it was difficult to shoot them with a .22 – now illegal – because if you missed you could quite easily kill some OAP having a sunbathe in Church Knowle, or Kingston for that matter. The only place you could shoot one without killing or injuring a civilian was on the Army firing ranges at Lulworth, to which the deer used to retreat when sated with rose shoots, knowing that access to them was forbidden. According to innumerable warning notices put up by the Ministry of Defence, trespassers ran a good chance of being blown to pieces, but in all the time we lived close by, the deer, as well as cows and sheep, continued to live there quite happily.

Our only defence was to use the sort of flashing lights that contractors put up when working on motorways. The deer didn't like them, but neither did we as they were expensive when bought in any quantity, and so were the batteries; also, unfortunately, the badgers loved the flashings and so far as we could see (and we never actually saw a single badger in all the years we lived there) they probably used to make up little parties for grub eating under the benevolent light of the flashing lamps.

Gradually, we learned all sorts of interesting things about West Bucknowle. Some time after the last war the house became a mini loony bin – only large enough for three or four inmates – which was occupied by the more genial, semi-loonies, male only, of the upper class. One of them was said to have run away with the proprietor's wife.

This previous history didn't bother us when we began to live there, simply because the house and its surroundings were so beautiful that we were constantly stopping whatever we were doing in order to admire them. There were the great beds of daffodils and bluebells, and the roses and the hydrangeas which all did so well here; the large back lawn that led through the tunnel of trees towards Kingston church, which I used to enjoy cutting with a mower in lovely, parallel swathes; and the big field two hundred yards or so long and up to fifty yards wide that ran down from the front of the house to the road, a field which had to be cut twice a year with a harvester.

But we could ill afford to dally for long simply because there was so much work to do. Ditches had to be cleared, a lot of dead timber had to be sliced up, there were coppices to be coppiced, and the apple orchard to be mown using a rough-cutter. There were also almost literally endless brambles, most of them growing from both ends, to be pulled up in the beech wood. This wood ran down steeply to the banks of the little Corfe River, which sometimes overflowed its banks; it had its source on the flanks of the Purbeck Hills and eventually emerged in Poole Harbour.

The biggest upset to all our efforts was the great hurricane of 1987, of which – as you looked at a map – our wood was on the extreme left flank. Although we were not sorry to see two immense Macrocarpa fall, they in their turn took down half a dozen great beeches, which, piled one on top of another when they fell, looked as if the Great Wall of China had been dumped in our back garden. In spite of all this, the tree tunnel, with its vista, survived.

Our neighbours were the Tennents. John Tennent was a noted ornithological painter. Their house overlooked a wild wood, the abode of large numbers of owls. It was built on the site of what had been the stables of our house; and it had probably also housed the sleeping quarters for the domestic servants who worked at West Bucknowle House, as there was no room for any servants there.

The Isle of Purbeck, which we had come to live on, is the tail end of Dorset, a little world almost entirely surrounded by water, most of it salt: to the north by the 10,000 acres or so of Poole Harbour and the River Frome; to the east by the approaches to the Solent, between the mainland and the Isle of Wight; to the south by the English Channel; and to the west by the Luckford Lake, a stream that you could probably jump across if chased by a bull. Unfortunately this stream just fails to end up in the sea near Lulworth Cove, so the title 'Isle' isn't really justified, but who cares?

Purbeck begins at Wareham, a market town and one-time seaport, most of it rebuilt in brick and local stone after a big fire in the 1760s. It stands, almost invisible from the outside, behind high grass ramparts built when Alfred was having trouble with the Danes in the ninth century, and strengthened in 1940 when George VI was having trouble with Hitler. The railway station, now the epicentre of a slight semi-industrial mess, is outside the walls.

To reach the town from it you cross over one of the two rivers which enclose it: the Piddle or Trent, and the Frome. The bridge over the Piddle – you can call it the Trent if you wish – has a cast-iron plaque, which warns: 'Anyone damaging this bridge will be transported for life. By order T. Fooks, Clerk of the Court.' There are several such cast-iron plaques with the same messages on bridges in other parts of Dorset (at Wool and Bridport for example), and they remind us that Dorset was a rough place for the proletariat in the not-so-distant past.

Dorset was the home of the Tolpuddle Martyrs – six farm workers sentenced to seven years' transportation for forming a trade union at Tolpuddle in 1834. The Soviet ambassador used to visit the village each year on the anniversary of the event. And in 1685 the western rampart of Wareham, known as Bloody Bank, was one of the places of execution of supporters of the Monmouth Rebellion, who were sentenced to death by Judge Jeffreys.

The name of the river, the 'Piddle or Trent', as the Ordnance Survey map puts it, reflects the indecision of the local bureaucrats who changed Piddletown into Puddletown, Affpiddle and Turner's Piddle into Puddles, but inexplicably reprieved Piddlehinton and Piddletrenthide, where 'I be going to Piddle' is still said to be the cry of the more elderly local commuters.

Just inside Wareham's northern ramparts, and practically scooped out of them, is the church of St Martin's-on-the-Wall. There is a deep whiff of antiquity about this place – not surprising as it is more than a thousand years old. In it, under a high timbered wood roof is a recumbent statue by Eric Kennington of T. E. Lawrence, killed riding his giant Brough motor cycle in a Dorset lane. This life-size stone effigy – he is dressed in Bedouin clothes, his right hand resting on the golden dagger of Mecca given him by Emir Hussein – is a work of genius.

From the church – originally the town had eight – the road to Purbeck leads through the town to a quay on the River Frome, Wareham's other river, where it is spanned by an ugly bridge. There, down by the warehouses that stand on the left bank of the river, is the Church of St Mary's. On its tower there's a weather vane in the form of a fish which was used as a shipping mark. It is from a little square nearby that you get your first sight of Purbeck across the water meadows. Constable would have enjoyed painting this view if he had come on here from Salisbury around 1831 when he painted Salisbury Cathedral from its meadows. Beyond the meadows, which have probably been meadows since the Middle Ages, is the Heath, otherwise the Heth, part of what Thomas Hardy called Egdon, the 'heathy, furzy, briery *Bruaria*' of Domesday – or what is left of it now that the Forestry Commission has planted huge numbers of conifers and the oil men have moved in.

Beyond this rather Teutonic wilderness – the comparison with the dark, coniferous woods in which I had lived in Germany as a prisoner during the last eighteen months or so of the war was irresistible – the land became more friendly. Here, under the lee of the Purbeck Downs – with their hanging woods and spinnies of ash and gnarled oaks – it was easy to fall in love with these hills and the houses which were hidden away among them.

Here, or anywhere we wanted to, we could climb up on to the Downs. None of them were much more than 600 feet high, most between 300 and 400. It was like being on the keel of a ship that had turned turtle. Up there the world was mostly sky populated in ever decreasing numbers by skylarks, kestrels and stonechats.

And up there you felt that you could see for ever: eastwards to the Isle of Wight, a real island; and westwards to Portland, like Purbeck a not quite real one, an isle joined to the mainland by Chesil Bank, a narrow sixteen-mile-long bank of shingle on which the stones increase from the size of a pea at the Bridport end to pebbles three inches in diameter at Portland. The pebbles provided sling-shots for the defenders of the nearby Iron Age fort of Maiden Castle, itself a wonder. As they get larger the bank becomes higher, steeper and wider. Here sometimes finds of ingots and coins are made, and it is a place of stranding for exotic fish – a merman was once reported as thrown up on it. All we ever found were coils of nylon rope with oil on them.

To the west is Flower's Barrow, on Ring's Hill, a truly amazing Iron Age fort on the edge of a 600-foot chalk cliff which still covers more than 15 acres, in spite of a third of it having fallen into the sea. When these falls happen the sea offshore becomes as white as milk.

From the Barrow we could look down on one of the great views in southern England: enfilades of chalk cliffs plunging to the sea, and rising from it, like a switch-back. And beyond them, down near the sea there is a forest of fossilized trees, and beyond that, like a great sea monster breasting the English Channel, the Isle of Portland, almost treeless, from which the stone came to build St Paul's Cathedral, the Bank of England, the Ministries in Whitehall – those colossal symbols of Edwardian Imperial optimism – and, hewn from its own small, personal quarry, the Cenotaph. Here, on Portland, half a million headstones were cut and carved with the names of the dead on the Western Front, together with the memorials for the war cemeteries, and 800,000 similar stones and memorials were cut in the nine years between 1947 and 1956. And there were the convicts, who first of all had to build their own accommodation, most of them brought to Portland en route for transportation to Australia and Tasmania. They built the huge breakwaters which were to make Portland Harbour the greatest artificial harbour in the world (2,130 acres), and the fortifications too.

In the twenty-two years between 1849 and 1871, the convicts cut 5,731,376 tons of rock, 2,000 of them working at a time, a norm of 1,500 tons a day, all of which was brought to the edge of the cliffs above the naval base and lowered down an inclined plane. The Prince Consort inaugurated the harbour by dropping a 9-ton chunk of stone into the water. Later he presented a Bible to each prisoner to encourage their repentance. Edward VII was less sanctimonious: he ordered treacle pudding for them, all round.

This was just part of a grand design. Beginning in 1849, to counter a possible invasion by Napoleon III, an enormous fort, Fort Victoria, 53 acres in extent, was built on the summit of the highest point of Portland, the Verne. By the time they had completed this truly awful work, the convicts – 3,000 of them at a time – had been made to cut a dry ditch through the living rock, 70 feet deep and 120 feet wide, removing 1½ million tons of material and making and laying 3 million bricks in the process, which were used to line the casemates.

What we saw on Portland resembled a rock-strewn battlefield fought over by giants of the Industrial Revolution – the ammunition being huge piles of squared-off stone, for some reason never used for the purpose for which they were intended.

There were the remains of mineral tramways, and railways that had once carried fare-paying passengers round the isle in long, serpentine curves; and there were cranes that were cranked by hand and the remains of other, unidentifiable, machinery; and there were fathoms of rusty wire rope that appeared to be growing out of the ground like iron weeds. In an almost treeless landscape alders were among the few trees there were. And there were powder magazines – tunnels, their mouths choked with thorns, that looked as if they might be housing within them a minotaur or two. And there were gun emplacements in which howitzers had been mounted capable of hurling 9.2-inch projectiles on to the decks of enemy dreadnoughts in the harbour below. And there were still various secret establishments and a grim Borstal institution (later a Youth Detention Centre); and a convict prison; and quarries, altogether about a hundred of them, huge enough to hide an army in. 'These are Imperial Works,' someone wrote at the time, without intentional irony, 'worthy of a Queen.' Not many convicts escaped from Portland. One who did get away was caught because he lacked a half-penny to buy a ticket on the ferry to the mainland.

Looking at this unearthly landscape it is difficult to believe that far into the second half of the nineteenth century, in spite of the quarrying works, life on Portland was largely pastoral and agricultural. There were cattle, and thousands of a breed of dark-faced sheep with curved horns that made them look as though they were wearing ear-trumpets. Portland mutton was regarded as the finest available. On Portland, women, the wives and daughters of the quarrymen and fishermen, worked what were thousands of strip fields. Cow dung was the staple fuel. Lumps of it were dried on the outer walls of the houses, and in the absence of other liquid fertilizers urine was used.

There was scarcely any crime, scarcely any infidelity – most of the people had been ardent Methodists ever since Wesley visited Portland in 1746 and preached there. A marriage was never solemnized until the girl was pregnant, and if this failed to happen the couple parted and started again with a new partner.

To get to the workable, what was called merchantable stone, thirty feet below the surface, was a Herculean task for quarrymen equipped with little more than hammers, wedges, pick-shaped tools called 'kivels', hand-operated cranes and Portland jacks – primitive instruments of a sort that, used in concert, could move up to 200 tons of rock horizontally along a quarry bed. The way to these merchantable beds was through ten levels of what are known, geologically, as the Lower Purbeck Beds – Shingle, Slat, Bacon Tier, Aish (used for holystoning the wooden decks of ships), Soft Burr, Dirt Bed (which yields fossilized conifers), Top and Skull Cap. Most of the stone from these levels was fit for nothing but to be thrown over the cliffs, to form what are now the mighty pile-ups at the foot of them. Only then did they reach the Portland Freestones – six distinct merchantable levels, most of which was dressed on site.

Up here, on the top of Portland, Weymouth – 600 feet below on the mainland, with its shopping centres and amusement arcades – seems a world away. Only the villages in which the quarrymen and their families lived, and some still do live, have a real feeling of humanity – villages such as Wakeham and Wester Green, with their cottages facing one another across main streets as wide as a motorway, or back to back. Here the people are happy to say good morning, or it's a nice day, even if their idea of a nice day is a bit different from ours, coming from the mainland.

These Purbeck Hills, the chalk hills we lived below at West Bucknowle, have grass-grown tumuli on them. Those on Nine Barrow Down to the east of Corfe Castle are the tombs of prehistoric notables. And there are dozens, if not hundreds of similar ones, all the way up to the Wiltshire border and beyond.

As the sun set on Flower's Barrow up on Ring's Hill, and the colours drained away, and the only sounds were those made by the sea dragging on the shingle in Worbarrow Bay hundreds of feet below, it was not difficult to believe that the phantoms of Vespasian's Second Roman legion, which finally subdued the area around Dorchester between A D 43 and 47, could be seen and heard marching towards Ring's Hill. And walking as we often did along the hills at night under a big moon, on Knowle Hill and Stonehill Down and Ridgeway Hill, neither of us would have been surprised to have encountered an apparition, although we would not have relished the idea. The most ghostly walk on these hills at night was along the wind-blasted southern side of Great Wood, above the hamlet of Steeple, which looked as if it had been shaved with a razor, to the Grange Arch, a Gothic folly with a long vista down through Great Wood to Creech Grange, a part-Palladian house of the Bond family, one of whom, in 1684, began the development of what became known as Old Bond Street, its pale limestone glittering in the moonlight.

A mile to the east of where we lived at Bucknowle, in one of the only two real gaps in the Downs between Ballard Down and Ring's Hill, are the colossal ruins of Corfe Castle. Built on a grassy mound of astonishing steepness, Corfe signifies a 'cleft in the hills'. It was at Corfe that the sixteen-year-old Edward, King of the English, was murdered, stabbed by order of his stepmother Elfthryth. One chronicler, Henry of Hunting-don, says she stabbed him herself while handing him a stirrup cup of wine while he was still on horseback. His corpse was taken to a miserable cottage on the Wareham road. And later he was to become Edward the Martyr. Elfthryth was so voluptuous that King Edgar, the so-called Peaceful, a red-headed midget, slew her husband in order that he could marry her. He was murdered because Edgar had employed him as a sort of marriage broker but the researcher had found Elfthryth so tempt-ing that he submitted an adverse report on her to the King and then married her himself. Eventually Elfthryth ended up in a nunnery, her body covered with white painted crosses in order to confuse the Devil. The murder of Edward was intended to facilitate the succession of his half-brother, the thoroughly incompetent Ethelred II, the Unready, to the throne. And in the reign of King John (1199–1216), who had a hunting lodge on Creech Hill, twenty two French knights were starved to death in the castle's dungeon on his orders. Edward II was also imprisoned here before being foully murdered at Berkeley Castle while a prisoner there in 1327.

In the Civil War, from 1642 to 1649, Corfe Castle was besieged by Roundheads who battered it with cannon balls, to little effect, receiving in return showers of rocks and red hot embers and ordures on their roundhead noddles, a defence ably led by Lady Bankes, its chatelaine in her husband's absence. He was elsewhere, fighting for the King. Eventually a treacherous Colonel Pitman opened a postern gate and the castle was taken. Its towers were so wonderfully constructed that when the victors undermined them and proceeded to blow them up with gunpowder – a process known as 'slighting' – many of them simply slid a few feet downhill, and remained intact, and remain so to this day.

The village below the castle was and is all that an English village can aspire to be, almost too perfect. There is an abundance of little shops selling door-knockers and other not so olde brasse objects, and teapots inscribed, 'If you're up to the neck in hot water just think of the kettle and sing.' And there is a good pub, the Fox Inn, which has very strong beer and a bar parlour the size of a pocket handkerchief, with a coal fire in winter. *Our* home pub was the New Inn at Church Knowle, one of the old New Inns in which Britain abounds.

Corfe also has a minute, one-room, eighteenth-century town hall in which the Company of Purbeck Marblers and Stone-Cutters held court on Shrove Tuesday. The church bell of King Edward the Martyr was rung, apprentices offered the Warden two pint tankards of beer, a penny loaf and six shillings and eightpence – what used to be a lawyer's fee for an opinion – for admission to the mysteries, the articles of which dated back to 1651. The meeting was concluded by the booting of a football across the 'Halves', a field through which the stone used to be carried on its way to a quay at Ower on the shores of Poole Harbour. At Ower a pound of pepper was presented to one of the inhabitants to safeguard the ancient right of way. That no stone has been shipped from Ower since 1710 is unimportant. The stone was limestone. The worked beds were at Langton Matravers between Kingston and Swanage, and below the cliffs between St Aldhelm's Head and Tilly Whim, near Swanage.

The whole of this area is honeycombed with workings. 'If some of the people putting up bungalows only knew what's underneath, they'd run for it,' a very old quarryman once told me with gloomy relish. 'We've taken the bowels out of it'; but nobody yet has had to run for it.

'First they sank a shaft, forty-five degrees or more, right through vein after vein, until they found what they wanted.' This was Mr Bowers speaking, member of a prolific family of quarrymen – there were also some quarrywomen. I met one once, a polisher. 'What they wanted was the Purbeck Marble,' continued Mr Bowers:

> That's the stuff. None left now you can get at easy. Half the cathedrals of England have it for the pillars and the old Crusader tombs – you can see them in Salisbury and Kingston, in the church there, long shafts of it, some of the last to be brought out. It's brown some of it and where the air gets to it, but otherwise it's a beautiful greeny blue and in columns six feet high, and by God it takes a polish! But it's all fossil shell, and you've got to be careful for it bruises, but when you've finished with it it's as blue as the sea itself.
>
> Then there was the Rag, no use. The Lannen Vein, the older men worked that. Blue Ragstone, too hard. Freestone, two sorts Thornback and Roach, that split as clean as a whistle, used for paving-stones. Then, right underneath, the Cliff Vein, Portland Stone, the sort they built Whitehall with, but harder to work than the Island stuff. How did they do it? Sixty feet down they made a 'lane' [a gallery], propping the roof with a 'leg' of cut stone as they went, shuffling along with their knees under their chins, propelling themselves forwards in the darkness with their knuckles.
>
> Then, by the light of a single candle, they cut out a block and hauled it out to the shaft on an 'elm cart', a trolley with solid wheels, on which one man could shift a ton. Then, with the block lashed to it with chains, an old pony hauled it to the surface, pulling on a long pole called a 'spack', which worked a wooden capstan with a six-foot-diameter drum. Now, mostly, they use bulldozers to get at the Freestone, used for tombstones and bird baths.

Below the ridge, out beyond Worth Matravers, are the tremendous cliffs on the sea coast, filled with disused workings such as Tilly Whim and Dancing Ledge and Seacombe Cliff and Winspit, below Kingston – mysterious workings, as mysterious as Egyptian rock tombs. One houses a colony of rare bats – or did, until recently. A coastline which to the west beyond St Aldhelm's Head at Chapman's Pool, is succeeded by a stretch of weird black shale cliffs full of fossil ammonites, all of them cliffs that are falling into the sea. They also yielded *Pliosaurus grandis*, a reptile with a 7′ head, a 6′ 9″ forepaddle and 13″ teeth.

One of the reasons why so much of Purbeck has remained undeveloped is because the Army took a chunk out of it 3 miles wide and 4½ miles deep during the Second World War for a tank firing range, dispossessing families who had lived in it and farmed it for countless generations. In spite of having promised to do so, the Army never gave it back. Their memorial is the ruined village of Tyneham – for centuries home of the Bonds – down in the valley that leads to Worbarrow Bay at the foot of Ring's Hill.

On the western edge of Purbeck, below Ring's Hill, is Purbeck's other castle, Lulworth. In 1929 it was burned by workmen, and until it was recently rebuilt, remained a beautiful, silver grey shell, with a round tower at each of its four corners with trees shooting up inside through what had been its roof, and jackdaws flying in and out of its gaping windows – a wonderful ruin. In the fire perished the great bed of George III, with its domed canopy, gilt crestings and royal blue hangings.

The castle had been home to the Catholic Welds, and in its grounds is the first Roman Catholic church to be built in England since the Reformation. 'Very well,' said George III, down at Weymouth for some sea bathing, to the senior Weld, Thomas, with whom he was staying. 'You can build a Catholic chapel but don't make it look like one.' So Weld commissioned a beautiful pagan temple with a superb altar, a sky-blue dome, and imported Italian stone workers from Italy to build it. Apparently the King gave permission because he was so entranced by the rendering of 'God Save the King' given by the assembled Weld children when he set off across the sands for his first dip in the waters of Weymouth Bay.

The long valley in which West Bucknowle stands at the foot of the Downs is green, black-and-white Friesian dairy country of hidden hamlets and some old churches – Church Knowle, Kimmeridge and Steeple. The church at Steeple displays heraldic devices belonging to the Lawrences of Creech Grange; over the door is a panel emblazoned with a shield-of-arms, the motif of which is actually part of the Stars and Stripes, the Lawrences being collateral ancestors of George Washington. But let us leave it to the genealogists to work out the degree of collateral relationship. The last Lawrence died in 1700, thirty-two years before George Washington was born.

At the far eastern end of this valley, which ends on the shores of a magnificent bay, is Purbeck's seaside resort, Victorian/Edwardian and 1930s Swanage. A resort to which I award the title of the 'Most Eccentric in the British Isles'. Paul Nash's description of it as 'perhaps the most beautiful natural site on the South Coast, ruined by generations of "development" prosecuted without discrimination or scruple' is equally true, if less endearing. Of all the painters who had a right to speak adversely of Swanage and Dorset Paul Nash, who really loved them, was the one.

Where else, beside the seaside, could you find the seventeenth-century façade of the Hall of a City Livery Company – in this case Mercer's Hall in Cheapside – incorporated in a Town Hall of 1882? Or an 1844 archway from Hyde Park Corner in the grounds of a mock-medieval, High-Victorian house? Or a clockless clock tower, a memorial to the Duke of Wellington, brought from its original site at London Bridge and rebuilt on a foreshore among fishing boats and lobster pots? Or a War Memorial commemorating King Alfred's victory over the Danes in 877, when their ships foundered on a reef off Peveril Point? A column surmounted, rather oddly, for a battle fought in 877, by four cannon balls. All these, together with the cast-iron street bollards and lamp-posts with the names of London parishes embossed on them, which are all over the place, were brought from London to Swanage as ballast for the ships that had taken Purbeck stone to London by the building contractor John Mowlem and his nephew, George Burt. One of the larger stone artefacts that never made it to London was a great stone globe of the world that weighed forty tons.

Even when we came to Purbeck, soon after the war, like the Divers in Fitzgerald's *Tender is The Night*, when they discovered the pleasures of sitting on the beach at Cap d'Antibes, thereby changing the habits of succeeding generations – no one had ever sat on a beach on the Riviera before – we decided that this was where we wanted to be.

But I had been in Purbeck before that, just as I had been in Swanage before that. It was Easter, 1927, when I was seven, or thereabouts, that I made what was for me a memorable journey on foot from Swanage to Tilly Whim Caves, while we were staying in Swanage.

My parents in rubber mackintoshes, my father wearing a large, floppy tweed cap, my mother wearing a close-fitting hat of the sort she used for motoring, and myself dressed in a regulation navy gabardine rain-coat, hatless, we headed off out of our boarding house, Rocklands Private Hotel, into the prevailing blast along Cluny Crescent and up Grosvenor Road, past the Suvla Bay and Wooloomoloo which were other boarding houses. Then, by what a sign described as unadopted roads, in the sense that they were full of pot-holes, we came to some rustic steps which led to the Belle Vue Hotel. There, already very damp, we drank hot Bovril from thick white porcelain mugs with Bovril inscribed on them.

It took me a long time to drink my Bovril as I was in a state of hysterics, being convinced that Belle Vue was really Belly Vue, until, rather sharply, my father told me to pull myself together.

Leaving this, to me, oddly named establishment, we followed a path grandly named on one of the innumerable stone slabs that were lying about all over the place as Isle of Wight Road. It was a weird spot, a wilderness through which Isle of Wight Road passed, a green, strangely quiet tunnel, sheltered by blackthorn and bramble, above which a mighty wind from the sea battered and tossed the branches of the ilex, the tamarisk and the huge pine trees, weird but enchanting. And I was full of excitement, scouting ahead, armed with a cap pistol, trying to read the inscriptions on London lamp-posts and bollards that sprouted sur-realistically from the all-embracing vegetation. Trying to decipher on stone slabs the names of roads built to serve Edwardian bijou houses that had never been built, like some manic antiquary, oblivious to the driving rain. And we went downhill to Durlston Castle with imitation machicolations and what looked like a conservatory stuck on one side of it. It seemed pretty feeble to me after other castles I had already visited: Windsor, Carisbrooke, Pevensey and what would be Corfe Castle, too, when we got around to it. The castle and the Great Globe were shut. In fact the whole place was shut, apart from the path we were now following downhill, hemmed in by blackthorn, tamarisk, and elder, made impregnable by bramble entanglements which I felt might conceal within them some hidden place, more wonderful than any of the above-mentioned castles, in which a beautiful princess might be sleeping for a thousand years. And in the middle of it was a battered and very ancient notice with the words inscribed on it: *No Sporting Dogs Allowed. Beware of Spring Guns!*

We continued downhill, past lines of funereal bollards linked by over-size wire ropes thick enough to support a suspension bridge, and came out on a sort of belvedere high above the sea on the edge of the cliffs where the full force of the gale hit us.

Huge seas were breaking at the foot of the cliffs and the air was full of rain and salt-tasting spray and the cries of sea birds (herring gulls, fulmars, kittiwakes and guillemots, although I didn't know what they were then and am not sure that I haven't got them wrong now). It was, as my father said, a jolly good place for deep breathing to clear the nasal passages, and while I inhaled a few ritual lungfuls he read out a poem, inscribed on yet another stone slab, the provenance of which I have never been able to identify, possibly written by the person who wrote the poem which begins 'Most noble Burt . . .' on another stone:

> An Iron Coast and Angry Waves
> You seem to hear them rise and fall
> And roar, rock-thwarted in the bellowing caves
> Beneath the windy wall 149 feet above sea level.

I liked the bit about the bellowing caves.

The entrance to the caves was by way of a locked iron gate between two stone pillars. A notice, as peremptory as the one to the poachers armed with spring guns, indicated that the caves were dangerous due to falling rock and that trespassers trespassed at their peril, which seemed a bit unfair as a succession of stone slabs inscribed *To the Caves* had been leading us on to them ever since we left Swanage.

Beyond this first gate there was another in the mouth of a dark hole, originally much more ponderous than the first one, but now almost rusted away. This one was not locked.

'Well, let's have a look at them,' said my father, to whom prohibitory notices of any sort acted as a red flag to a bull, already beginning to scramble around one of the pillars where the earth had eroded.

'Oh, George, do you think we ought to?' said my mother.

'I've not come all this way for nothing,' he said, sentiments with which I whole-heartedly agreed, helping her over the obstructions.

The second gate opened with a reluctant screeching sound; beyond it an inclined shaft led to the depths below. It was pitch-dark and a freezing wind blew up it, bringing with it the boom of the sea. Underfoot the shaft was clay on rock, horribly slippery.

In such circumstances there was no point in trying to hold an adult hand. The adults had as much as they could cope with, anyway. It was obvious that if one of them fell, the others would be brought down also. With my repeating cap pistol at the ready, half hoping that there might be smugglers or signs of smugglers down below, and half hoping there wouldn't be, I followed my father gingerly down, one hand on a slimy wall. I saw him trying to light matches with a conspicuous lack of success, and half expected him to disappear from view in some man-made oubliette. My mother even more gingerly brought up the rear, occasionally calling, 'George, are you all right?'

Then it grew lighter and there was another terrible screeching noise as my father pushed open a third gate. The noise of the sea was deafening. The wind almost strong enough to lean on, and then, suddenly, we were on a ledge above the sea, which was breaking over it in clouds of spray.

Above us, on an enormous rock, which formed part of the cliff, was yet another inscription:

> The cloud-capped towers, the gorgeous palaces,
> The Solemn temples, the Great Globe itself,
> Yea, all which it inherit, shall dissolve.
> And like this insubstantial pageant faded,
> Leave not a rock behind.

Which I thought was rather good, although I didn't understand much of it, and my father read it well.

Now we were turning a corner, threading our way between huge boulders, getting drenched by a sudden cloud of spray. From this side, at that time, it was easy to enter the caves. There were no gates at all. Beyond us was a narrow gulf in which the sea raged. High above on a cliff, barely visible in the mist, there was a squat lighthouse half hidden behind white-painted walls with its light flashing. And as we stood taking in this scene, there was a loud explosion.

'That's the fog signal,' my father said, after the first explosion, dispelling a faint hope that it might have been produced by smugglers. Visibility was only a couple of hundred yards. It was, it seemed to me, good smugglers' weather.

'I didn't see any signs of smugglers,' I said. Although I was enjoying my first day at Swanage it was difficult not to conceal my disappointment about the absence of smugglers.

'That doesn't mean that there aren't any,' my father said, resting a hand lightly on my shoulder, in a way that he intended to be reassuring and was. 'Smugglers only work at night, and they don't leave any traces behind them.'

Slowly we began to climb the steep path up the cliff, the easy way. So far, apart from the woman who had served us the Bovril at the Belle Vue, we had not seen another human being.

INDEX